A Student's Companion to Old Irish Grammar

Ranke de Vries

CONTENTS

ACKNOWLEDGMENTS

I would like to thank Damian McManus, Jürgen Uhlich, Peter Schrijver and Justin Gregg very much for their helpful comments on earlier drafts of this work.

I compiled the handouts that form the basis of this book during my time as a teaching assistant at Trinity College Dublin. The information contained in them was based in part on discussions during the lectures I myself attended there (especially Jürgen Uhlich's grammar course), and it would therefore have been impossible to compile this book without the inspiring lectures of Liam Breatnach, Damian McManus and Jürgen Uhlich. You have managed to make early Irish grammar not only understandable, but enjoyable. I can only hope to attain the same.

FOREWORD

Back when I was teaching my very first tutorial in Old Irish grammar as a Ph.D. student, it became clear quite early on that students wanted more information about grammatical subjects than was found in the books that we were working with. As a result of this, I decided to write handouts for them that explained in more detail what had been discussed during class, in hopes that it would help the students understand the underlying patterns better.

This book, a reworking of those handouts, which I have deliberately written in a very colloquial style, is intended for those who approach Old Irish as a new language without a background in historical linguistics. You can use this book on its own, but also in conjunction with the other grammar books out there. Old Irish is a beautiful language, but it can be daunting at first, so in my view the more grammar books you can consult as you learn it, the better.

In this book, you will find a general overview of the most important grammatical themes and concepts. There are in fact many exceptions to the overview given here, but if I were to discuss them here, I fear it would only confuse the reader, which would be counter-productive; and in any case, for those interested, these exceptions are usually discussed elsewhere in detail.

Originally, the handouts followed the order of Quin's *Old-Irish Workbook* (the book used in the grammar classes at Trinity College Dublin), but in order to make this book more user-friendly, I have rearranged the topics in what I hope is a more logical order, and an order that is easier to consult quickly (this is also the reason why the table of contents is so expansive).

In order to make it easier to use this book in combination with other works out there, I have added references to seven other grammar books currently in use at different universities to the beginning of each topic (beginning at the chapter on the article) for ease of reference. These are: (1) R.P.M. and W.P. Lehmann's *An introduction to Old Irish* (New York 1975), referred to below as 'Lehmann'; (2) Kim McCone's *A first Old Irish grammar and reader including an introduction to Middle Irish* (Maynooth 2005; this is referred to as 'McCone'); (3) E.G. Quin's *Old-Irish workbook* (Dublin 1975, referred to as 'Quin'); (4) David Stifter's *Sengoídelc: Old Irish for beginners* (Syracuse, NY 2006, referred to as 'Stifter'), (5) John Strachan's *Old-Irish paradigms and selections from the Old-Irish glosses* (Dublin 1949, referred to as 'Strachan'), (6) Rudolf Thurneysen's *A grammar of Old Irish, revised and enlarged edition* (Dublin 1946, reprint 1993, referred to as '*GOI*')[1] and (7) Wim Tigges in collaboration with Feargal Ó Béarra, *An Old Irish primer* (Nijmegen 2006, referred to as 'Tigges').

Occasionally, you may notice that some of the text is in smaller print. In the case of paradigms (so the lists containing the different forms of certain words), this is simply in order to be able to fit a table on one page, but if this happens in the main text, the parts in smaller print are there to give you extra information – you may choose to skip this when you read the book for the first time.

---

[1] The reason I refer to Thurneysen's grammar as *GOI* is because this is the way that people usually refer to it in other works.

BEFORE WE BEGIN: BASIC GRAMMATICAL TERMS

The purpose of this section is to explain some very commonly used grammatical concepts to you that you may not be familiar with. It is divided into two parts. The first part will focus on phonology and orthography (in other words, it has to do with sounds and spelling); the second part of the section deals with syntax (sentence construction). If you are already familiar with the subjects discussed below: great! Feel free to skip the entire section. If you are not yet familiar with them: no problem at all. You certainly will be by the end of the book. It is likely that you will encounter the grammatical concepts and terms discussed here very often throughout this book and in any other works of Old Irish grammar, so it is crucial that you understand them and familiarize yourself with them.

A. Phonological and orthographical concepts

Vowel and consonant

Sounds are represented in writing by either a vowel (generally speaking a sound made with an open vocal tract)[2] or a consonant (a sound in which there is constriction of some part of the vocal tract). There are also things called semi-vowels or demi-vowels, i.e. *w* and *y*, that I am ignoring for now in order to avoid confusion. The **vowels** written in Old Irish are: *a, e, i, o, u*, and they can be short or long (in which case they have a length-mark on them, so *á, é í, ó, ú*; note that these lengthmarks are often omitted in the manuscripts); **consonants** are *b, c, d, f, g, (h,) l, m, n, p, r, s, t.*

It is crucial to note that in Old Irish, **these letters can represent different sounds**, depending on for example where they stand in a word. The pronunciation of Old Irish can be daunting at first, but do not despair. This will get better with practice. I will first provide a basic, slightly simplified, overview of the pronunciation of consonants, then of vowels.[3] The pronunciation is indicated between these brackets: // and I will try to approximate the pronunciation where possible in British English – but bear in mind that these are only approximations!

---

[2] The vocal tract is a term used for the area in the body where the sounds produced in your larynx can be filtered or modified.

[3] Stifter gives a more elaborate discussion which you may well want to read for yourself – see Stifter: 15-24.

1

letter	pronunciation at beginning of word[4]	pronunciation between vowels/ as final letter after vowel
p	/p/ (as *p* in 'pen')	usually /b/ (as *b* in 'ball'), but occasionally /p/
t	/t/ (as *t* in 'ten')	usually /d/ (as *d* in 'dog') but occasionally /t/
c	/k/ (as *c* in 'cat')	usually /g/ (as *g* in 'mug'), but occasionally /k/
b	/b/ (as *b* in 'bone')	usually /β/ (as *v* in 'vase') but occasionally /b/
d	/d/ (as *d* in 'dog')	usually /ð/ (as *th* in 'then') but occasionally /d/
g	/g/ (as *g* in 'get')	usually /γ/,[5] but occasionally /g/
m	/m/ (as *m* in 'mug')	usually /ṽ/[6] but occasionally /m/
r	/rr/[7]	/r/
l	/ll/	/l/
n	/nn/	/n/
f	/f/ (as *f* in 'foot'),	/f/
s	/s/ (as *s* in 'soot')	/s/

Now, for the vowels. The pronunciation of the vowels in Old Irish depends on whether the syllable in which the vowel is found is **stressed** or **unstressed**. The term 'stressed' here basically means that it is pronounced louder, with more energy than the others.

---

[4] That is, the letter is the first letter of a word (this position is sometimes called *anlaut*); if the letter in question stands in word-final position (in other words, it is the last letter of the word), it is sometimes said that the consonant stands in *auslaut*. In this overview, the first letter is not lenited or nasalized; for lenition and nasalization, see the section on 'mutations' below).

[5] This sound is pronounced in the back of your throat by pressing the back of your tongue against the soft palate (also called *velum*). It is found in a number of different languages like Modern Greek, Spanish or in the south of the Netherlands, but for those of you not from there and not familiar with this sound, Stifter explains it very well as the voiced counterpart to German /ch/ (so you pronounce it like the *ch* in *Bach*, but then by vibrating your vocal chords – see Stifter: 19).

[6] This sound is a nasal *v*; that is to say, while you are pronouncing it, you are letting air escape simultaneously through both your mouth and nose.

[7] The *r* is a rolling *r*, like you might find in Spanish or Welsh; the difference in pronunciation between /rr/ and /r/, as well as the difference between /ll/ and /l/ and /nn/ and /n/ is that the /rr/, /ll/ and /nn/ are pronounced longer and in a larger area in the mouth than /r/, /l/ and /n/.

2

The stress in Irish words is usually placed on the **first syllable** of the word, although there are exceptions: there are for instance a (fair) number of unstressed words (i.e. they do not have any stress). An example of an unstressed word is the negative particle *ní* 'not', used with verbal forms. And not only that: there are also words in which the stress lies on the second syllable (e.g. *ar**aile**, 'another', where I have written the stressed syllable in bold letters; and this stress on the second syllable business is standard practice in certain types of verbs – but no worries for now, we'll get to that later).

Please note that if you see a length-mark on a vowel (this looks like an acute accent), this just means that a vowel is long. It does NOT automatically mean that the syllable in which it occurs is stressed! Basically, the vowels are pronounced normally if they are in stressed position, and all vowels except *u* are pronounced as 'uh' in unstressed position.[8] This 'uh' sound (called *schwa*) is often represented in grammars by the symbol ə:

letter	pronunciation in stressed position	pronunciation in unstressed position
A	/a/ (as *a* in 'father')	/ə/ (as the *e* in 'father')
E	/e/ (as *e* in 'let')	/ə/
I	/i/ (as *i* in 'in')	/ə/
O	/o/ (as *o* in 'morning')	/ə/
U	/u/ (as *ou* in 'you')	/u/ (as *ou* in 'you').

Diphthongs
In words, you may encounter a sequence of multiple (usually two) vowels. Sometimes, these vowels are combined in pronunciation, and produce one syllable – this is called a diphthong. The diphthongs in early Irish are: *aí/áe, oí/óe, ía, uí, au, áu/áo, eu, éu/éo, íu, ou, óu, úa.*[9] Some examples: *Móen* (personal name), *cóeca* 'fifty', *cíall* 'sense'.

Hiatus
In addition to the diphthongs, there are also words in which two vowels that stand next to each other are not combined in pronunciation, but are pronounced separately, as two syllables. This pronunciation break is called hiatus. A hiatus is often indicated in editions of texts by putting two dots (if

---

[8] The vowel written in an unstressed syllable depends on the color or quality of the surrounding consonants (see below for a discussion of what 'consonant color' is) – for the rules, see Stifter: 22 or McCone: 16.

[9] Note however that *au, ou* and *eu* are replaced by *u* fairly early on.

3

you like fancy terms, this is called *diaeresis*) over one of the two vowels (usually the second vowel, e.g. *oäc* 'young'). Hiatus is mainly found in early texts – it starts to disappear in the Old Irish period and vanishes altogether in Middle Irish.

Prefixed 'h'
Sometimes you find the letter 'h' attached to the first letter of a word that begins in a vowel. This 'h' is called 'prefixed'. Most commonly you will find it in front of a small word like *ed*, 'it', for example to distinguish it in the manuscripts where lots of words were written together to save space. This 'h' is not pronounced (in contrast, there is a sound /h/ that is produced by something called *h*-mutation, mentioned below, although that, confusingly, is not usually written).

Consonant color
(also called *consonant quality*)
The pronunciation of a consonant in Old Irish originally depended on what vowel followed it. If a consonant was followed by an *o*, *a* or *u*, it was pronounced normally. In grammar books it usually says that the consonant in that case has a **neutral color or quality** (also called **broad**). The *o* and *a* are sometimes called **neutral** (or **broad**) vowels.

If a consonant was followed by an *i* or an *e*, people would already start forming that *i* or *e* with their mouths (by raising the center of the tongue towards the roof of the mouth, otherwise known as the palate) while they were still pronouncing the consonant that came before it. The result of this was that the consonant would sound slightly differently. Grammar books call this a consonant with a **palatal quality or color** (sometimes also a **slender** consonant). If you see the vowel *i* in a word, it almost always means that both the consonant following it and the one preceding it are palatal (example: the genitive singular of *fer* 'man', namely *fir* 'of a man', where both the *f* and the *r* are palatal). The vowel *e* generally means that the preceding consonant is palatal, but that the following consonant is neutral, e.g. *fer*, 'man', where the *f* is palatal, but the *r* is neutral (you can see this in the Modern Irish word *fear* 'man'). The vowels *i* and *e* are sometimes called **palatal** or **slender** vowels.

For those who have never heard of this: a palatal consonant is pronounced almost as if you add the letter *j* to it. This is the easiest way for me to explain it. Try it. Add the letter *j* to a palatal consonant, and then pronounce the *j* so fast that you can barely hear it.

Another way of determining whether a certain consonant or consonant group is palatal or not is by looking at the *glide vowels*.

Glide vowels

In Old Irish words, we often find something called a **glide vowel**. Glide vowels are there to help you (isn't that nice?). They are always placed between a consonant and another vowel (or vice versa), and their only function is to indicate either that the consonant that follows it is palatal or that the consonant which precedes it is neutral or palatal. Glide vowels are not pronounced.

Notes: In early sources, glide vowels are often absent, and this can lead to confusion. For example, the word *berid*, without a glide, can either mean 'he carries', or 'he may carry'. In the first case, 'he carries', the *r* is palatal; in the second one, 'he may carry', the *r* is neutral. By adding an *i*-glide in the first case (giving you *beirid* 'he carries') it is much easier to distinguish between these forms.
On a sidenote, The expression 'he may carry' is often spelled *beraid*, with *–ai–* after the *r*. This *a* is **not** a glide, however – it is one of the ways in which to represent an unstressed vowel between a neutral and a palatal consonant – see McCone: 16 and Stifter: 22.

There are three glide vowels in Old Irish: the *i*, *e* and *a*. The *i* is the only one that is found in two cases. It can (1) be added to a word to indicate that the consonant following it is palatal, e.g. *beirid*, where the glide tells you that the letter *r* that follows it is palatal; and it (2) can be placed between a consonant and a final unstressed *u* to indicate that the consonant in front of the *u* is palatal, e.g. *Ériu* 'Ireland', *gaibiu*, 'I take'.

The *e* and *a* are found between a consonant and a final unstressed vowel. In the case of the *e*, the glide is inserted between a palatal consonant and the neutral vowels *o* or *a*, e.g. *cairtea* 'friends'. The *a*-glide is inserted between a neutral consonant and a palatal vowel (*e* or *i*), e.g. *lámae* 'of a hand'. Remember – this is important:

Glide vowels DO NOT REPRESENT SOUNDS. They are not considered to be real vowels and are not themselves pronounced; their **only function** is to indicate consonant color.

Syncope

In Old Irish texts, you will often encounter something called *syncope*. Very simply put: if a syllable was added to a word in Old Irish that already consists of two syllables, the vowel of the second syllable was lost. This loss of the vowel is called *syncope* (from Greek, literally meaning 'cutting together' – two syllables are thrown together because something has been cut out). The easiest way to remember this is by thinking of **2 + 1 = syncope**. Most commonly, this happens when you add an ending to a noun or a verbal stem.

Now a very tricky point, so pay attention:

> The **color** (palatal, neutral) of the (original) vowel that is lost determines the color of the consonant (group) that remains.

This means that if you lose a palatal vowel (an *i* or an *e*), the consonants that surrounded that vowel remain (or if they were not yet palatal, are made) palatal. If you lose a neutral vowel (*a*, *o*), the consonant group remains/becomes neutral.

An example: the word *claideb*, 'sword' consists of two syllables. If you put *claideb* in the dative plural, you have to add the ending *-(a)ib*. The *a* between brackets is is used if the consonant before it is neutral. The outcome that you might expect would be something like **clai-deb-(a)ib*. But as you can see, **clai-deb-(a)ib* has three syllables. So what do we get? That's right, syncope! As I have already said, syncope means that you lose the vowel of the second syllable. In this case, that is the letter *e*. As we have seen, *e* is a palatal vowel, so the consonants around it (*d* and the *b*) will be(come) palatal. The outcome is therefore *claidbib*.

Notes:
1) If a word had more than five syllables, syncope of the fourth syllable occurred - but we do not have that many words in Old Irish that are that long. See for example *GOI* § 106.
2) Above, I wrote 'the color of the **original** vowel that is lost determines the color of the consonant (group) that remains. I had to say original, because the Old Irish word *carpat* 'chariot' has an acc. pl. *cairptiu*. This seems odd at first glance – the vowel lost seems to be an *a*, so one might expect to get dat. pl. **carptu*. But when one knows that the original vowel lost was palatal (as evidenced in other Celtic languages, such as Gaulish *carpentum*) the palatalisation of *–pt–* makes sense. The second *a* in *carpat* reflects a weakened pronunciation of the second syllable, since that was unstressed.

Mutations
In all insular Celtic languages, you will find a phenomenon called **mutation**. This means that in specific cases and circumstances, words or word-endings can 'mutate' a following word, most often the initial sound of a following stressed word. This 'mutation' affects the pronunciation of that initial sound - though this is not always reflected in the spelling of these letters. Note: **unstressed words** like the particle *ní* **cannot** (generally) be mutated.

Mutations can occur in connection with nouns, but also with certain verbal forms in certain constructions.

There are a number of types of mutations: **lenition** (in early sources this is sometimes called 'aspiration'), **nasalization** (sometimes called 'eclipsis'), and **h-mutation**[10] and **gemination**; the ones that are most important for you here are lenition and nasalization. Usually, these mutations affect small groups of words that belong together (e.g. groups consisting of a noun and an adjective or a noun followed by a genitive, for example 'the house of a warrior'). The main obstacle with mutations is that in Old Irish, you usually cannot tell from looking at a word whether it will cause a mutation or not. You will have to learn what mutations occur where, when and why (o thrill, o joy).

A very brief background for those interested:
In earlier stages of the Irish language, such as Primitive Irish, it was actually a lot easier to predict when a word would cause a mutation, because back then the nouns still had real endings. An example: the nominative singular of the Old Irish word *fer*, 'man', goes back to Primitive Irish * *wir-ah* and Proto-Celtic *wir-os*, with the ending *–os*. Generally speaking: words that in Proto-Celtic ended in a *vowel* would start to *lenite* the initial of the following word, words that ended in a *nasal* would *nasalize* the initial of the following word, words that ended in a vowel + *-s* would cause *h-mutation* if the next word would begin in a vowel (the reason for this being called h-mutation rather than something like s-mutation is that the *–s* first changed to *–h* in pronunciation); any other letter did nothing. These endings were lost or at the very least severely reduced at the end of the Primitive Irish period through a process called *apocope* (again Greek, literally 'cutting off'). Because of this apocope, by the time Old Irish came around, you could not tell anymore simply from hearing a word what it was going to do. For more information on this, you can turn to Stifter, or, if you know Modern Irish, Kim McCone's chapter on Old Irish and its prehistory in *Stair na Gaeilge*; see also McCone's *Towards a relative chronology of ancient Celtic sound change*.

1. Lenition

Lenition is the only kind of mutation that can occur both at the *beginning* of a stressed word and *inside* a word. Basically, lenition is the shorter or fricative[11] pronunciation of a consonant through the influence of surrounding vowels. To put it very simply: if a consonant stood after a vowel, it would be lenited. This goes for both consonants in a word and for consonants at the beginning of a word.

---

[10] Stifter calls *h*-mutation 'aspiration', so be careful that you don't confuse this with lenition.
[11] That is, a sound produced by forcing air through a small passage, for example the *f* in 'father'.

Lenition at the beginning of a word originally (in the Primitive Irish period and before) occurred when the preceding word ended in a vowel. In the middle of the word, lenition basically occurred when a consonant stood between two vowels. An example of this is *máthair*, 'mother', where '*t*' has been lenited to '*th*' because it stands between two vowels.

In Old Irish, lenition can only be seen in the spelling of a few consonants: *c, t, p, f* and *s*. Lenited *c* is spelled *ch* (*mo chenél* 'my kindred'); lenited *t* becomes *th* (*a thech*, 'his house'); *p* becomes *ph* (*a Phátraic* 'O, Patrick'); lenited *f* and *s* are spelled with a dot over it, *ḟ* and *ṡ* (*a ḟir, a ṡacart* 'his man, his priest'). This dot is called a *punctum delens* ('deleting point'). Lenited *f* (*ḟ*) is not pronounced. When a lenited *s* (*ṡ*) is preceded by the sound -*t* (for example *int ṡúil*), it is not pronounced, but in all other cases lenited *ṡ* is pronounced /h/.

Lenition of other consonants was not yet reflected in writing in Old Irish, although it was expressed in pronunciation (for example, a lenited *b* would still be written as *b*, but pronounced as a *v*, lenited *d* was pronounced as /ð/, lenited *g* as /γ/, lenited m as /ṽ/).

Note: In medieval manuscripts, lenition of *c, t, p* can be indicated by writing out the following *h*, but it is very often indicated with a spiritus asper (which basically looks like a check mark above the letter), and sometimes it is accidentally omitted. The letters *f* and *s* often have the *punctum delens*, but sometimes, especially in later manuscripts, may have the *h* written out, or it may be missing there as well.
Lenition of *b,d,g* and *m* is indicated in later manuscripts, usually either by placing a *punctum delens* over it, or by adding *h* (so *bh, dh, gh* and *mh* would be written respectively to represent lenited *b, d, g,* and *m*).

Delenition
There is a phenomenon that occurs in Old Irish called *delenition*. This means that a sound that should be lenited isn't. Delenition occurs when a consonant that is supposed to be lenited stands next to a **homorganic consonant** – that is, a consonant that is pronounced in the same place in your mouth. One of the instances where it happens is when a nasal (*n* or *m*) is followed by the sound *d* or *t*.

An example: take the verbal form *glantae*, 'you (pl.) clean'. The regular ending of the second person plural absolute would be *–thae*, but because the *n* and the *t* are both pronounced in the same place in your mouth (try it!), you get delenition. Delenition often happens as a result of syncope.

2. Nasalization

Nasalization only occurs at the beginning of a stressed word (or stressed part of a verb). The reason for nasalization dates back to (Proto-Celtic and) Primitive Irish: when the preceding word would end in a nasal (*n* or *m*) it would nasalize the initial of the following word (or, to put it differently: you would still be forming the nasal with your mouth as you were starting to pronounce the next sound). Of course, in Old Irish, we do not have these endings anymore, so again we have to learn when exactly nasalization will occur.

In Old Irish, nasalization is written out before only a few letters: *b, d, g* and any vowel (becoming *mb, nd, ng* and *n-V* respectively, where *V* stands for any vowel). In all other cases it is just pronounced. Again, in later times, scribes start to write out this nasalization, which is why in Modern Irish you have spellings like *bhf* for nasalized *f, gc* for nasalized *c, dt* for nasalized *t* and *bp* for nasalized *p*. Nasalized *b* becomes *mb* in Old Irish (e.g. *inna mbríathar* 'of the words'), *d* becomes *nd* (e.g. *a ndliged*, 'the law'), *g* becomes *ng* (*a ngalar*, 'their sickness') and a nasalized vowel has the letter *n* before it, usually separated from the vowel by a dash or hyphen in modern editions (*inna n-ech*, 'of the horses').

3. H-mutation

This mutation is only heard in pronunciation, and is not reflected in the spelling of words (you do sometimes find words beginning with the letter *h*, but this is not a reliable indication that h-mutation has actually taken place – see also above under 'prefixed h'). H-mutation is, very generally speaking, found in Old Irish after words ending in a vowel that do not lenite or nasalize, and a 'h' is pronounced if the following word begins with a vowel (for example the possessive pronoun 3 sg. feminine, *a*, 'her', causes h-mutation, so the word *ech* in the phrase *a ech* 'her horse' is pronounced as 'hech' (/heχ/).

B. Syntactical concepts

Subject
The subject of a sentence is the person/animal/thing who performs the action, so *the man* walks the dog; *Fiona* falls down.

Direct Object
A direct object (often simply referred to as 'object') is the person/animal/thing that undergoes the action: the man throws *the ball*, Fiona sees *a film*.

Indirect Object
The indirect object is the person/animal/thing to or for whom/which something is done: he writes a letter *to me*.

Verb
A verb is a word that denotes an action or state in a sentence, e.g. the man *walks* his dog, the girl *talks* to her friends, my sister *is* here, I *attend* a tutorial. It can come in six different **persons**: the first person singular ('I'), the second person singular ('you'), the third person singular ('he/she/it'), the first person plural ('we'), the second person plural ('you'), the third person plural ('they').

A verb can also come in different **tenses** (times, if you will), i.e. present tense, past tense and future tense, and in different **moods**, i.e. indicative (generally indicating reality, as in 'you see'), subjunctive (generally indicating things that are not real (yet), but for example a wish or possibility, 'you may go' or 'you can go') and the imperative (generally indicating an order, e.g. 'go!').

There is one very important thing to remember:

> In Old Irish, when the **subject** of the sentence is a **personal pronoun** (that is, *I, you, he, she, it, we, you* or *they*, (e.g. *you* walk, *he* sees etc.)) these pronouns are **included in the verb form itself**, much like the word *táim*, 'I am', in Modern Irish. In Old Irish they do not yet have the forms we use now in Modern Irish or in English, with independent pronouns that stand separated from the verb, like Modern Irish *tá mé, tá sí*, 'I am, she is' and English **he** *is* etc.

Word-order

A sentence in Irish (as well as the other Celtic languages) has a different word-order than that found in English and many other languages. In English, the most common word-order is Subject-Verb-Object-everything else (some people therefore call this an **SVO-language** — note that 'Object' here refers to the direct object). Irish is different, as you may well know from Modern Irish. The usual word-order in Irish is Verb-Subject-Object-everything else (a so-called **VSO-language**).

Noun

A noun is a word that denotes a thing, place, person or abstract notion, e.g. a man, a dog, a vase, a house, love, kingship. In Old Irish, nouns are divided into different groups according to different stem classes, for example *o*-stems and *u*-stems. When looking at a noun, there are three things that you should pay attention to: what is the **gender** of the noun, what is the **number** of the noun and what is the **case** of the noun.

Case

In the Old Irish that we are studying, and indeed still in modern Irish, there are five cases: the **nominative, vocative, accusative, genitive** and **dative**.

The **nominative** case is generally used to denote the **subject** of a sentence, that is, the person or thing that performs the action in that sentence: *the man* runs, *the dog* barks, *the vase* breaks.

The **vocative** case is used when you **address someone**, e.g. '*Pete*, come over here!' '*Dad*, where is the coffee?' In Irish this case is (almost) always accompanied by a special word (called particle) *a*; so if you were to address St. Patrick, you would say *a Phátraic*.

The **accusative** case is often used to denote the **(direct) object** in a sentence. The direct object is the person or thing that is affected by the action in a sentence, i.e. the dog bites *the man*, the man drops *the letter*, the girl climbs *the Eiffel tower*. In addition, the accusative case is used after certain prepositions (e.g. into, onto — see also below).

The **genitive** case is used to qualify another noun, usually by expressing **possession**, e.g. *the man's* hat, the cat *of my mother*, or by expressing the more general idea of 'part, of something', e.g. a crock *of gold*, the end *of the day*.

The **dative** case in Old Irish is virtually always preceded by certain prepositions, and it is therefore very easy to translate as the translation depends on the meaning of these prepositions. Occasionally, you will find a noun in the dative case that does not have a preposition in front of it. This is called an 'independent dative'. This independent dative is found most often in (very) early prose and poetry; it can have four different meanings.

As Stifter points out,[12] the use of the term 'dative' is somewhat misleading since that which is called the dative case in Old Irish actually unites what used to be four distinct cases: the **dative**, expressing a so-called indirect object, that is *to whom* or *for whom* something is destined, e.g. 'he gives *me* a book, she writes a letter *to her mother*'; it can have an **instrumental** meaning (*with what*, e.g. 'he killed the man *with a frying pan*'), an **ablative** meaning (*away from whom/what* 'she ran *from his house*') and a **locative** meaning (*at/by what/whom* 'the well is located *at the crossing* of two roads').

Gender
In Old Irish, a noun can have three genders: **masculine**, **feminine** and **neuter**. The neuter is usually reserved for objects, not persons.

Number
There are three different numbers that the noun can have: **singular**, **plural** and **dual**. The singular denotes 'one, a single', e.g. a (single) man, a (single) dog. The plural denotes 'more than two', e.g. men, women, schools. The dual, as you may have guessed, denotes 'two', e.g. two men, two dogs. In Old Irish the dual is always accompanied by the word for two - so it is generally easy to spot!

Adjective
An adjective says something about a noun, so: a *blue* house, a *sunny* sky, a *terrible* day. Adjectives in Old Irish take the same gender and case as a noun, and stand in the singular if the noun is in the singular, and in the plural if the noun it accompanies stands in either dual or plural.

Adverb
An adverb further qualifies a verb or an adjective. In English, this is usually marked by adding the ending *–ly* to an adjective, for example: 'the heist went *terribly* wrong' (further qualifying how wrong exactly that heist went); 'he sobbed *uncontrollably*', 'they suffered *greatly*' (qualifying a verb, and possibly saying something about students of Old Irish who has seen the section on the verb for the first time). In Old Irish, an adverb is usually formed by placing the adjective in the dative singular, usually preceded by the article (e.g. *in biucc* 'little', *in már* 'greatly'). There are a few examples in Old Irish of an adverb being formed by placing the preposition *co* 'until'

---

[12] Stifter: 37. He refers to this case as 'prepositional case'.

before the adjective (compare this with Modern Irish *go minic* 'often').

Preposition
A preposition is a word that generally indicates a place or direction, and it is used in conjunction with a (pro)noun. When I first learned about prepositions some three decades ago, my teacher gave us a memory aid which I have always found very helpful: if you put prepositions in front of 'the cage', prepositions will provide you with information of an object in relation to that cage, so '*in* the cage, *to* the cage, *from* the cage, *through* the cage, *between* the cage and something else, *around* the cage' etc. Prepositions in early Irish are followed by either the dative or accusative case.

And now, high time to get started! Fasten your seatbelts, because it might get a bit bumpy at times. If you find you are having a hard time understanding certain concepts, or if you are beginning to despair and think you will never be able to learn Old Irish (this happened to me the first time I took a class on Old Irish grammar), try to remember that everybody who is currently teaching Old Irish has had to learn it just like you: it can be done. It really helps to repeat what you have learned, so review often – and never be afraid to ask for help if things are unclear. Chances are, you are not the only one who is having a difficult time.

I. THE ARTICLE

(*GOI*: §§467-73; Lehmann: 36-7, 62-3; McCone: 33-6; Quin lessons 4-5; Stifter: 39, 50-2, 62-3, 379; Strachan: 1; Tigges 26, 51)[13]

In English, there are two kinds of articles. There is the **indefinite article** 'a', which you use if you say 'a man', 'a dog', 'a school' etc. and there is a **definite article** 'the', which you use when you say 'the man', 'the world', 'the scary-looking red alcoholic drink.'

In Old Irish, **you only find the definite article**. The indefinite article **does not exist**. If you want to say 'a man' in Old Irish, you just say *fer*.

In Irish, the article always comes before the noun (as opposed to certain languages like, say, Swedish, where the article follows the noun).

As is the case with nouns, the definite article can take different cases, genders and numbers. The article always has to be in the **same case, gender and number as its accompanying noun**. For example: if you see a noun in the genitive plural masculine, the article in front of it stands in the genitive plural masculine as well. Some forms of the article mutate (lenite, nasalize etc.) the initial of the following word.

IMPORTANT NOTE:

> Just because an article causes a certain mutation, that **does not mean** that the noun following it will! An example: the article genitive singular masculine lenites the following noun, but whether the noun that follows is going to cause lenition or not, depends entirely on what stem the noun belongs to, since there are masculine nouns that have a genitive singular that does not lenite (see below in the section on the noun). So beware. Or, to borrow the adage of Alistair 'Mad-eye' Moody from the Harry Potter series: CONSTANT VIGILANCE!

Let's dive in, shall we?

---

[13] References to Lehmann, McCone, Stifter, Strachan, Tigges are to page numbers; references to Quin are to lessons, and references to Thurneysen (the *GOI* entries) are to paragraph numbers.

I.a. The pattern for the article

Note: Wherever you find the form *inna*. in texts you may find *na* instead of *inna*. This is just a shorter form. In the overview here, you will find this as *(in)na*. You may also notice that there is no form of the article for the vocative (hurray!).

Pattern of the article masculine – singular

Case	Form of the article	Mutation[14]	Explanation
Nom.	*in fer* 'the man' *in macc* 'the son/boy' *int én* 'the bird' *int ech* 'the horse'	none	The form *int* is used if the next word begins in a vowel; in ALL other cases, *in* is used
Acc.	*in fer* 'the man' *in n-ech* 'the horse'	nasalizes	The form *in* is ALWAYS used. But remember: not all letters that are nasalized show nasalization! Note also that in the accusative case certain combinations of preposition + article are found, such as *lasin fer* 'with the man'
Gen.	*in chéili* 'of the fellow' *ind fir* 'of the man' *int ṡailm* 'of the psalm'	lenites	The form *int* is used when the next word begins with lenited *s* (usually spelled *ṡ*); *ind* is used if the next word begins in a vowel, lenited *f* (*f*), *l*, *r* or *n*. *In* is used in ALL other cases. Note that delenition may take place if the noun following the article begins with a ho-morganic consonant (e.g. *in toíb* 'of the side,' where *n* and *t* are homorganic).
Dat.	*don*[15] *chéiliu* 'for the fellow' *cosind euch* 'with the horse' *dont ṡalm* 'to the psalm'	lenites	As in gen. sg., you find *-nt* before lenited *s* (*ṡ*), *-nd* be-fore a vowel or lenited *f* (*f*), *r*, *l*, *n* and *-in* in ALL other cases. The article in the dat. sg. is (almost) always found

---

[14] With 'mutation' I mean: what does this form do to the following word if possible (will it lenite it, nasalize it, or cause h-mutation)?

[15] Since the dative article is (almost) always combined with a preposition, I have done so here as well.

combination with a preposition (see I.c. below). As in gen. sg., delenition may take place (e.g. *don tóeb* 'to the side')

Pattern of the article masculine – plural

Case	Form of article	Mutation	Explanation
Nom.	*in* *chéili* 'the fellows' *ind* *fir* 'the men' *int* *sailm* 'the psalms'	lenites	see gen. sg.
Acc.	*(in)na* *firu* 'the men' *(in)na* *echu* 'the horses'	h-mutation	Form *(in)na* is used in all cases. When combined with a preposition only *–na* is used, e.g. *lasna firu* 'with the men'
Gen.	*(in)na* *fer* 'of the men' *(in)na* *n-ech* 'of the horses'	nasalizes	Form *(in)na* is used in all cases.
Dat.	*do***naib** *feraib* 'for the men' *do***naib** *echaib* 'for the horses'	none	The article, of which only the ending *(s)naib* is visible is found in combination with certain prepositions.

Pattern of the article masculine - dual

The article in the dual is not often used in texts. For the dual, the article in the nom., acc. and gen. is *in*, for the dative in combination with a preposition it becomes *don* 'for the', *isin* 'in the', *ón* 'from the' etc. Remember that the dual is always accompanied by the word for 'two', *dá* in the nom./acc./gen. dual, *dib* in the dative plural. The article *in* would theoretically cause lenition, but because *dá* begins with the letter *d*, delenition occurs, as *n* and *d* are homorganic consonants:

Case	Form of article	Mutation
Nom.	*in* *dá ech* 'the two horses'	*dá* lenites the following word
Acc.	*in* *dá ech* 'the two horses'	*dá* lenites the following word
Gen.	*in* *dá ech* 'of the two horses'	*dá* lenites the following word
Dat.	*do***n** *dib n-echaib* 'for the two horses' *co***sin** *dib n-echaib* 'with the two horses' etc.	*dib* nasalizes the following word

Pattern of the article feminine – singular

Case	Form of article	Mutation	Explanation
Nom.	*in túath* 'the tribe'[16] *ind lám* 'the hand'	lenites	same rule applies that you have seen in gen.sg. and nom.pl. masculine: *int* if followed by lenited *s* (*ś*), *ind* if followed by lenited *f* (*f́*), *l, r, n* or a vowel; *in* in all other cases
Acc.	*in túaith* 'the tribe' *in n-insi* 'the island'	nasalizes	in all instances *in* is used
Gen.	*(in)na túaithe* 'of the tribe' *(in)na céille* 'of the sense'	h-mutation	in all instances *(in)na* is used
Dat.	*don túaith* 'for the tribe'* *cosind láim* 'with the hand'	lenites	see pattern for dat. sg. masculine

Pattern of the article feminine – plural

Case	Form of the article	Mutation	Explanation
Nom.	*(in)na túatha* 'the tribes', *(in)na lama* 'the hands'	h-mutation	in all instances *(in)na* is used
Acc.	*(in)na túatha* 'the tribes', *(in)na cíalla* 'the senses'	h-mutation	in all instances *(in)na* is used
Gen.	*(in)na túath* 'of the tribes' *(in)na ndelb* 'of the shapes'	nasalizes	in all instances *(in)na* is used
Dat.	*donaib túathaib* 'for the tribes' *donaib delbaib* 'for the shapes' etc.	h-mutation	in all instances *(s)naib* is used in combination with prepositions

Pattern of the article feminine - dual
The numeral 'two' in the feminine nominative and accusative is *dí*. This word lenites the following initial.

Case	Form of the article	Mutation
Nom.	*in dí thúaith* 'the two tribes'	*dí* lenites the following word
Acc.	*in dí thúaith* 'the two tribes'	*dí* lenites the following word
Gen.	*in dá thúath* 'of the two tribes'	*dá* lenites the following word

---

[16] Note the delenition of the initial *t-* in *túa(i)th* because *n* and *t* are homorganic consonants.

Dat.	**don** dib túathaib 'for the two tribes' etc.		**dib** nasalizes the following word

Pattern of the article neuter – singular

Case	Form of the article	Mutation	Explanation
Nom.	**a** cenn, **a** ndliged 'the head', 'the law'	nasalizes	in all instances *a* is used
Acc.	**a** cenn, **a** ndliged 'the head', 'the law'	nasalizes	in all instances *a* is used
Gen.	**in** chinn, 'of the head' **ind** éoin, 'of the bird' **int** síde, 'of the elfmound'	lenites	works exactly like the genitive singular
Dat.	**don** chiunn, 'for the head' co**sind** éun, 'with the bird' do**nt** síd, 'to the elfmound'	lenites	works exactly like the masculine and feminine feminine dative singular

Pattern of the article neuter - plural

Case	Form of the article	Mutation	Explanation
Nom.	**(in)na** cenél(a) 'the races'	h-mutation	in all instances *(in)na* is used
Acc.	**(in)na** dligeda, **(in)na** scéla 'the laws', 'the stories'	h-mutation	in all instances *(in)na* is used
Gen.	**(in)na** ndliged, **(in)na** cenél 'of the laws', 'of the races'	nasalizes	in all instances *(in)na* is used
Dat.	**donaib** dligedaib 'to the laws' **donaib** scélaib 'for the stories'	h-mutation	works exactly like dative plural masculine and feminine

Pattern of the article neuter - dual

Case	Form	Mutation	Translation
Nom.	**in** dá ndliged	*dá* causes nasalization	the two laws
Acc.	**in** dá ndliged	*dá* causes nasalization	the two laws
Gen.	**in** dá ndliged	*dá* causes nasalization	of the two laws
Dat.	**don** dib ndligedaib	*dib* causes nasalization	for the two laws

I.b. The double article rule

This brings us to a lovely concept called the 'double article rule':

> If you want to translate a (part of a) sentence from English into Irish, which consists of definite article + noun followed by definite article + genitive, i.e. '**the** hair of **the** man, **the** color of **the** cows, **the** falling of **the** rain,' you *only use one definite article in Irish*. This article stands before the **second** element, so 'the hair of the man' in Old Irish became *folt ind fír*, and NOT **in folt ind fír*. This is the same in Modern Irish (e.g. *dáth na rósaí*, 'the color of the roses').

Note: the article may also be omitted if the next element is very specific, like a personal name, e.g. *macc Conchobuir* 'Conchobar's son, **the** son of Conchobar' (as in, the only one). If you are wondering now how you would translate 'a son of Conchobar's' (as in, one of several), you would do this with the preposition *do*: *macc do Chonchobur*.

I.c. The combination preposition + article

In Old Irish, when a **preposition** is **followed by an article**, the preposition and the article are **combined**.

For all of you lucky enough to know Modern Irish, you already know this, because this also happens in Modern Irish! Think of the preposition 'in': if you want to say 'in the city', you say *sa chathair*; 'in spring' is *san earrach* – these are combinations of preposition + article. Some of you already know more than you think!

I mentioned in the overview of general grammatical terms that dative cases in Old Irish are (almost) always preceded by a preposition. If you want to say 'for the messenger' in Old Irish, the article would have to come after the preposition and before the noun. In this case, the basic form of the article would be *in*. You then might expect something in Old Irish that would look like **do in thechtairiu*. Unfortunately, you do not: the actual Old Irish translation of 'for the messenger' is *don thechtairiu*, in which the preposition and the article are combined. This is also the case in instances where a preposition is used that is followed by the accusative case. An example of that: if you want to say 'with the man', you can use the preposition *la* which is followed by a word in the accusative case. The outcome of this in Old Irish is *lasin fer*.

But now we have a problem: a mystery 's' just appeared! 'Where does it come from and why is it not there in our example *don thechtairiu*?' I hear you ask yourself (or at least you should be asking yourself this – if not, you have not been paying attention. In that case, I suggest you get yourself some coffee and read this section again).

A short explanation:
In Proto-Celtic (there we go again!), the article started with the letter *s* (the nominative singular masculine was *sindos*, for example; Stifter gives a wonderful overview of these forms). This *s* is the letter *s* that shows up in *lasin fer* – so it is a remnant of the original form of the article. So that is that question answered.

Now for the second question. That letter *s* (and we all know what it is now) disappears *if the preposition that is combined with the article* **lenites** *the following word.* The preposition *do* happens to cause lenition, so the *s* is lenited and disappears. *If a preposition causes h-mutation or nasalization, the letter 's' will be there.*

So when the prepositions *la*, 'with' which causes h-mutation, and *i*, 'in', which causes nasalization are combined with the article, you see the letter *s*. Examples: *lasin mball*, 'with the limb' *isin tempul* 'in the temple'. I shall provide you with an overview of prepositions and what they look like in combination with the article under the schedule for the pattern of the article below.

I.d. Overview of the most common prepositions + article
All prepositions are followed by words that stand in a particular case. Usually this is the dative or the accusative.[17] Some prepositions (such as the prepositions *i*, 'in', *ar*, 'for', *for*, 'on') are followed by either a dative or an accusative. These prepositions generally take the **accusative** if you wish to express **motion** (e.g. 'I walk *into* a room, I climb *onto* a horse'); they take the **dative** if you wish to convey a sense of **rest** (e.g. 'I am sitting *on* a carpet *in* a room').

NOTE: in the column 'preposition + article singular' you will sometimes see two forms. This occurs when the preposition is followed by the accusative case. The form ending in '–(*i*)*n*' is used if the preposition + article is followed by a *masculine or feminine noun*; the one ending in '–*a*' is used if it is followed by a *neuter noun*. If there is only one form, this means that it is the form used if the preposition + article can be followed by masculine, feminine and neuter.

---

[17] A few prepositions like *dochum* 'to' and *sechnón* 'throughout' are followed by a genitive case, but they are not very common.

	meaning	mutation	followed by	prep.+art sg.	+art. pl.
a	out of	h-mutation	dative	*asin(d/t)*	*asnaib*
ar	for, on	lenites	dative	*arin(d/t)*	*arnaib*
	for, onto	lenites	accusative	*arin, ara*	*arna*
co	with	nasalizes	dative	*cosin(d/t)*	*cosnaib*
co	to	h-mutation	accusative	*cosin, cosa*	*cosna*
do	for, to	lenites	dative	*don(d/t)*	*donaib*
fo	under	lenites	dative	*fon(d/t)*	*fonaib*
for	on	h-mutation	dative	*forsin(d/t)*	*forsnaib*
	onto	h-mutation	accusative	*forsin/forsa*	*forsna**
fri	against	h-mutation	accusative	*frisin, frisa*	*frisna*
i	in	nasalizes	dative	*isin(d/t)*	*isnaib*
	into	nasalizes	accusative	*isin, isa*	*isna*
la	with	h-mutation	accusative	*lasin, lasa*	*lasna*
ó	from	lenites	dative	*ón(d/t)*	*ónaib*

* These forms of the article combined with the preposition *for* can also occur without the letter *s* in them.

21

II. THE NOUN

In Old Irish, (almost) all nouns are declined. That means that for each **case** (nominative, vocative, accusative, genitive and dative), **number** (singular, plural and dual) and **gender** (feminine, masculine and neuter) the nouns take a different form. You can predict what a noun is going to look like if you know what **stem** (and number and gender) the noun belongs to. All stems have their own pattern. There are two general types of stems: **vocalic stems** and **consonantal stems**. First, we will a look at the vocalic stems.

II.a. Vocalic stems

The vocalic stems are so named – you'll never guess it – because (originally) the stem contained a certain vowel. Here is an overview of the different vocalic stems and what genders they can take. Note that not all stem classes contain words of all three genders! The term 'masculine' is abbreviated to m., 'feminine' to f., 'neuter' to n. The last class, diphthong, is only mentioned here because you find it in Strachan's *Paradigms*, and *GOI* discusses this word under the heading 'exceptions and indeclinable nouns', §340; it will not be treated below.

Stem	Gender	Example in Old Irish
o	m, n	*fer* 'man' (o, m)
		cenél 'kindred' (o, n)
io	m, n	*daltae* 'fosterson' (io, m)
		cride 'heart' (io, n)
ā	f	*túath* 'tribe', *cíall* 'sense'
iā	f	*guide* 'prayer', *soilse* 'light'
ī	f	*inis* 'island', *sétig* 'wife'
i	m, f, n	*cnáim* 'bone' (i, m), *súil* 'eye', (i, f), *muir* 'sea' (i, n)
u	m, n	*dorus* 'door' (u, m), *bith* 'world' (u, m), *rind* 'star, point' (u, n), *mind* 'diadem' (u, n)
diphthong		*bó* 'cow' (f)

II.a.1. *o*-stems

(*GOI*: §§276-80; Lehmann: 7, 8, 85; McCone: 23-6; Quin lessons 1-2; Stifter: 43-6 ; Strachan: 2-3; Tigges: 21-2, 54-5)

The *o*-stems are so called because (surprise!) originally these endings contained the letter *o*. The word *fer*, 'man', for example, comes from Proto-Celtic **u̯iros*, where *-os* is the ending. As you can see, there is an *o* there. Unfortunately, those endings were lost long before the Old Irish period. Since the endings are no longer there, this means that we all have to learn (or, less ideally, look up) what the stem of a certain noun is.

In the nominative singular, *o*-stems all end in a **neutral consonant or consonant group**.

There is one exception: *Día* 'God', is a (masculine) *o*-stem that originally ended in a neutral consonant, which it no longer had in Old Irish.

The *o*-stems can either be **masculine** or **neuter**. All the nouns of the *o*-stems follow a certain pattern (examples given are *fer* 'man' and *macc* 'son, boy' as well as *ech* 'horse', the latter so you can see the nasalization after *dib* in the dual):

o-stems masculine

Singular

Case	Form	Mutation	How to reconstruct	Translation
Nom.	*fer*	none	---	a man
	macc			a son
	ech			a horse
Voc.	*a fir*	lenites	last consonant palatalized*	o, man
	a maicc			o, son
	a eich			o, horse
Acc.	*fer*	nasalizes	looks like nom. sg.	a man
	macc			a son
	ech			a horse
Gen.	*fir*	lenites	last consonant palatalized	of a man
	maicc			of a son
	eich			of a horse
Dat.	*do fiur*	lenites	*u* is often added before	for a man**
	do macc		final consonant (group)	for a son
	do euch			for a horse

* This usually (though not always) means that the *i*-glide is stuck in right before the final consonant (group) – see the forms *maicc* and *eich*.
** The dative is almost always preceded by a preposition, as you know. In these

23

overviews, I have added a preposition (usually *do*) before words in the dative case, just like I did in the section on the article.

Plural

Case	Form	Mutation	How to reconstruct	Translation
Nom.	*fir*	lenites	last consonant is	men
	maicc		made palatal	sons
	eich			horses
Voc.	*a firu*		ending -*u* is added	o, men
	a maccu			o, sons
	a echu			o, horses
Acc.	*firu*		ending -*u* is added	men
	maccu			sons
	echu			horses
Gen.	*fer*	nasalizes	looks like nom. sg.	of men
	macc			of sons
	ech			of horses
Dat.	*do feraib*	none	ending (*a*)*ib* is added	for men
	do maccaib			for sons
	do echaib			for horses

Dual

Note: the vocative dual is not found in Old Irish, so in the overviews below it has been omitted.

Case	Form	Mutation	How to reconstruct	Translation
Nom.	*dá fer*	lenites	looks like nom. sg.	two men
	dá ech			two horses
Acc.	*dá fer*	lenites	looks like nom. sg.	two men
	dá ech			two horses
Gen.	*dá fer*	lenites	looks like nom. sg.	of two men
	dá ech			of two horses
Dat.	*do dib feraib*	none*	ending −(*a*)*ib* is	for two men
	do dib n-echaib		added	for two horses

* Pay attention however: while the noun does not cause a mutation, the word *dib* nasalizes the following noun (so the word *n-echaib* is nasalized because of *dib*, but *n-echaib* itself does not cause nasalization of the following word, e.g. *do dib n-echaib beccaib* 'for two small horses').

o-stems neuter

It is typical of neuter words that the nominative and the accusative (and in Old Irish the vocative as well) have the same form, so the nom., acc. and voc. sg. will all look the same; the same goes for the nom., acc. and voc. plural and for the nom. and acc. dual (we have no vocative dual in Old Irish, but if we did, it would have looked the same as the nom. and acc.

24

dual). Of course, in the vocative case, we always have that particle *a* or *á* which lenites, but the form of the noun itself is the same as that of the nominative and accusative. Examples are of *arm* 'weapon' and *cenél* 'race (of people)':

Singular

Case	Form	Mutation	How to reconstruct	Translation
Nom.	*arm*	nasalizes	---	weapon
	cenél			race
Voc.	*a arm*	nasalizes	looks like nom. sg.	o, weapon
	a chenél			o, race
Acc.	*arm*	nasalizes	looks like nom. sg.	weapon
	chenél			race
Gen.	*airm*	lenites	final consonant	of a weapon
	cenéoil		is made palatal	of a race
Dat.	*do arm*	lenites	*u* is inserted where	for a weapon
	do chenéul		possible	for a race

Plural

Please note that there are two different forms in the nominative, vocative and accusative plural of neuter *o*-stems. The shorter forms (*cenél* etc.) cause lenition and are generally used when there is no doubt that the meaning of the word is plural, e.g. if it is preceded by the number three: *trí chenél*, which obviously must mean 'three tribes'. If doubt could arise, the longer form is generally used, which does not cause a mutation.

Case	Form	Mutation	How to reconstruct	Translation
Nom.	*arm(a)*	lenites/none	looks like nom. sg./	weapons
	cenél(a)		ending –*a* is added	races
Voc.	*a arm(a)*	lenites/none	same as nom. pl./	o, weapons
	a chenél(a)		ending –*a* is added	o, races
Acc.	*arm(a)*	lenites/none	same as nom. pl./	weapons
	cenél(a)		ending –*a* is added	races
Gen.	*arm*	nasalizes	looks like nom. sg.	of weapons
	cenél			of races
Dat.	*do armaib*	none	ending –(*a*)*ib* is added	for weapons
	do chenélaib			for races

Dual

Case	Form	Mutation	How to reconstruct	Translation
Nom.	*dá n-arm*	nasalizes	looks like nom. sg.	two weapons
	dá cenél			two races
Acc.	*dá n-arm*	nasalizes	same as nom. dual	two weapons
	dá cenél			two races
Gen.	*dá n-arm*	nasalizes?	same as nom. dual	two weapons
	dá cenél			two races

| Dat. | *do dib*
n-armaib
do dib cenélaib | none | ending *–(a)ib* is
added | for two
weapons
for two races |

II.a.2. *io*-stems

(*GOI*: §§281-7; Lehmann: 42-3, 116; McCone: 23-6; Quin lesson 3; Stifter: 74-5; Strachan: 5; Tigges: 21-2, 54-5)

io-stems can be either masculine or neuter. They typically consist of more than one syllable (if you want to be fancy, you can call that *polysyllabic*) and in the nominative singular, they end in the letter *-e*. *io*-stems basically follow the same pattern as the *o*-stems – so *io*-stems masculine follow the same pattern as *o*-stems masculine (and *io*-stems neuter that of neuter *o*-stems). In those places where *o*-stems masculine have a final neutral consonant (nom., acc. sg., gen. pl. and nom., acc. and gen. dual), *io*-stems masc. end in *-e*; where *o*-stems masc. have a final palatal consonant (gen., voc. sg; nom. pl.), *io*-stems masc. end in *-i*; where *o*-stems masc. have a *-u*, (dat. sg., voc. and acc. pl.) *io*-stems masc. end in *-u*; the dative plural **always ends in a palatal *b***. Mutation patterns also correspond, so where *o*-stems lenite, *io*-stems will lenite etc. The pattern:

io-stems masculine
Singular

Case	Form	Mutation	How to reconstruct	Translation
Nom.	*céile* *daltae*	none	---	fellow fosterson
Voc.	*a chéili* *a daltai*	lenites	replace final *-e* with *-i*	o, fellow o, fosterson
Acc.	*céile* *daltae*	nasalizes	form looks like nom.sg.	fellow fosterson
Gen.	*céili* *daltai*	lenites	replace final *-e* with *-i*	of a fellow of a fosterson
Dat.	*do chéiliu* *do daltu*	lenites	replace final *-e* with *-(i)u*	for a fellow for a fosterson

Plural

Case	Form	Mutation	How to reconstruct	Translation
Nom.	*céili* *daltai*	lenites	replace final *-e* with *-i*	fellows fostersons
Voc.	*a céiliu* *a daltu*	none	replace final *-e* with *-(i)u*	o, fellows o, fostersons
Acc.	*céiliu* *daltu*	none	replace final *-e* with *-(i)u*	fellows fostersons

Gen.	*céile*	nasalizes	form looks like nom.sg.	of fellows
	daltae			of fostersons
Dat.	*do chéilib*	none	replace final *e* with -*(a)ib*	for fellows
	do daltaib			for fostersons

Dual

Case	Form	Mutation	How to reconstruct	Translation
Nom.	*dá chéile*	lenites	looks like nom.sg.	two fellows
	dá daltae			two fostersons
Acc.	*dá chéile*	lenites	looks like nom. sg.	two fellows
	dá daltae			two fostersons
Gen.	*dá chéile*	lenites	looks like nom. sg.	of two fellows
	dá daltae			of two fostersons
Dat.	*do dib céilib*	none	replace final -*e* with	for two fellows
	do dib ndaltaib		-*(a)ib*	for two fostersons

io-stems neuter

Singular

Case	Form	Mutation	How to reconstruct	Translation
Nom.	*cride*	nasalizes	---	a heart
Voc.	*a chride*	nasalizes	same as nom. sg.	o, heart
Acc.	*cride*	nasalizes	same as nom. sg.	a heart
Gen.	*cridi*	lenites	replace final -*e* with -*i*	of a heart
Dat.	*do chridiu*	lenites	replace final -*e* with -(i)u	for a heart

Plural

Case	Form	Mutation	How to reconstruct	Translation
Nom.	*cride*	lenites	form looks like nom. sg.	hearts
Voc.	*a chride*	lenites	form same as nom. pl.	o, hearts
Acc.	*cride*	lenites	form same as nom. pl.	hearts
Gen.	*cride*	nasalizes	form looks like nom. sg.	of hearts
Dat.	*do chridib*	none	replace final -*e* with -*ib*	for hearts

Dual

Case	Form	Mutation	How to reconstruct	Translation
Nom.	*dá cride*	nasalizes	form looks like nom. sg.	two hearts
Acc.	*dá cride*	nasalizes	form looks like nom. sg.	two hearts
Gen.	*dá cride*	nasalizes	form looks like nom. sg.	of two hearts
Dat.	*do dib*	none	replace final -*e* with -*ib*	for two
	cridib			hearts

II.a.3. ā-stems

(*GOI*: §§288-91; Lehmann: 14-5; McCone: 23-5; Quin lesson 5; Stifter: 59-61; Strachan: 3-4; Tigges: 21-2, 54-5)

Up to now, we have only dealt with masculine and neuter nouns (*o*-stems and *io*-stems), but now we finally get to deal with feminine nouns! **All nouns** that belong to the *ā*-stem are feminine. Nouns of *ā*-stems end in a neutral (broad) consonant (group) in the nominative singular. Here is the basic pattern for the *ā*-stems:

Singular

Case	Form	Mutation	How to reconstruct	Translation
Nom.	*túath*	lenites	---	a tribe
Voc.	*a thúath*	lenites	form looks like nom. sg.	o, tribe
Acc.	*túaith*	nasalizes	ending is made palatal	a tribe
Gen.	*túaithe*	h-mutation	*-e* is added	of a tribe
Dat.	*do thúaith*	lenites	ending is made palatal	for a tribe

Plural

Case	Form	Mutation	How to reconstruct	Translation
Nom.	*túatha*	h-mutation	*-a* is added to nom. sg.	tribes
Voc.	*a thúatha*	h-mutation	form looks like nom. pl.	o, tribes
Acc.	*túatha*	h-mutation	form looks like nom. pl.	tribes
Gen.	*túath*	nasalizes	form looks like nom. sg.	of tribes
Dat.	*do thúathaib*	none	ending *–(a)ib* added	for tribes

Dual

Case	Form	Mutation	How to reconstruct	Translation
Nom.	*dí thúaith*	lenites	ending is made palatal	two tribes
Acc.	*dí thúaith*	lenites	looks like nom.dual	two tribes
Gen.	*dá thúath*	lenites	form looks like gen.pl., but notice the different form of the numeral 'two' (*dá* instead of *dí*)!	of two tribes
Dat.	*do dib túathaib*	none	*–(a)ib* added to stem	for two tribes

NOTE: The genitive singular ends in the letter *–e*; often this means that the consonant group before it becomes palatal (for example in the gen. sg. of *túath*, 'tribe', *túaithe*; *cíall*, 'sense', *céille*), but not always (for example the gen.sg. of *lám* 'hand', *lámae*; *delb* 'form', *delbae*).

OTHER NOTE: Some words in this group contain the diphthong *–ía-* (for example *cíall*, 'sense'); when the endings of those words become palatal (dat. sg. and acc. sg., nom. and acc. dual) and in the gen. sg., the diphthong changes to –*éi*-, so *cíall* becomes *céille* and *céill*. If you do not remember what a diphthong is exactly, you can look it up in the discussion of general grammatical terms.

The pattern (also called *paradigm* – so now those of you who are using Strachan's book know why it is called (Old Irish) *Paradigms* – because you find the patterns for the different nouns and verbs in Old Irish in it) for the word for woman, *ben*, is irregular – and how! I would advise you to learn it, because it is one of those words that keeps popping up in texts. This is the pattern for *ben* (see also *GOI* §291, Stifter: 61; Strachan: 4):

Case	Singular	Plural	Dual
Nom.	*ben* (lenites)	*mná*	*dí mnaí* (lenites)
Voc.	*a ben* (lenites)	*a mná*	---
Acc.	*mnaí* (nasalizes)*	*mná*	*dí mnaí* (lenites)
Gen.	*mná*	*ban* (nasalizes)	*dá ban* (lenites)
Dat.	*mnaí* (lenites)*	*mnáib*	*dib mnáib*

* Very rarely, in early texts, the form *bein* is found here instead of *mnaí*.

II.a.4. *iā*-stems
(*GOI*: §§292-8; Lehmann: 42-3, 116; McCone: 23-5; Quin lesson 6; Stifter: 83; Strachan: 6; Tigges: 21-2, 54-5)

The relationship between *ā*-stems and *iā*-stems is pretty much the same as the relationship between *o*-stems and *io*-stems. The nominative singular of *o*-stems (which, as I have said, can be either masculine or neuter) and *ā*-stems (which are always feminine) ends in a **neutral or broad consonant**; whereas *io*-stems (again, these can be either masculine or neuter) and *iā*-stems (again, these are always feminine) consist of more than one syllable (i.e., are polysyllabic) and **end in the letter -*e*.**

With regard to *iā*-stems, you can say two things:

(1)   the mutation pattern is **exactly the same** as that for *ā*-stems. That means that the nominative, dative and vocative singular lenite, the genitive singular causes h-mutation, the accusative singular nasalizes, the genitive plural nasalizes, the nominative, vocative and accusative plural cause h-mutation, the dative plural does nothing, the dual nominative, accusative and genitive lenite and the dual dative does nothing (don't worry, I have put this down in a table to make it clearer).

29

(2) where the words of *ā*-stems end in *a neutral or broad consonant or in the letter -e* (that is, in the nominative, vocative and genitive singular, in the genitive plural and in the genitive dual), *iā*-stems end in the letter *-e*. Where the words of *ā*-stems end in a palatal or slender consonant with the exception of the dative plural (so in the dative and accusative singular and in the nominative and accusative dual), *iā*-stems take the ending *-i*. The nominative and accusative plural, which in *ā*-stems end in *-a*, end in *-i* in *iā*-stems. As always, the dative plural ends in a slender *b* (so *-aib* if the preceding consonant (group) is broad or neutral, *-ib* if the preceding consonant (group) is slender or palatal).

Now, in an overview with the examples *guide*, 'prayer' and *fairrge* '(open) sea, ocean':

Singular

Case	Form	Mutation	How to reconstruct	Translation
Nom.	*guide*	lenites	----	prayer
	fairrge			ocean
Voc.	*a guide*	lenites	looks like nom. sg.	o prayer
	a fairrge			o ocean
Acc.	*guidi*	nasalizes	final *-e* replaced with *-i*	prayer
	fairrgi			ocean
Gen.	*guide*	h-mutation	form ends in *-e*	of a prayer
	fairrge			of an ocean
Dat.	*do guidi*	lenites	final *-e* replaced with *-i*	for a prayer
	i fairrgi			in an ocean

Plural

Case	Form	Mutation	How to reconstruct	Translation
Nom.	*guidi*	h-mutation	final *-e* replaced with *-i*	prayers
	fairrgi			oceans
Voc.	*a guidi*	h-mutation	final *-e* replaced with *-i*	o prayers
	a fairrgi			o oceans
Acc.	*guidi*	h-mutation	final *-e* replaced with *-i*	prayers
	fairrgi			oceans
Gen.	*guide*	nasalizes	looks like nom. sg.	of prayers
	fairrge			of oceans
Dat.	*do guidib*	none	replace final *-e* with	for prayers
	i fairrgib		*-(a)ib*	in oceans

Dual

Case	Form	Mutation	How to reconstruct	Translation
Nom.	*dí guidi*	lenites	replace final *-e* with *-i*	two prayers
	dí fairrgi			two oceans

Acc.	*dí guidi*	lenites	replace final -e with -*i*	two prayers
	dí fairrgi			two oceans
Gen.	*dá guide*	lenites	form ends in -*e*	of two prayers
	dá fairrge			of two oceans
Dat.	*do dib nguidib*	none	replace final -*e* with -(*a*)*ib*	for two prayers
	do dib fairrgib			for two oceans

II.a.5. *i̯*-stems

(*GOI*: §§292-8; Lehmann: -, but *blíadain* treated under iā-stems) McCone: 23-5; Quin lesson 7; Stifter: 84-5; Strachan: 7; Tigges: 34)

As with *ā*-stems and *iā*-stems, words belonging to the *ī*-stem (also called 'long *i*-stems') are **always feminine**. The *ī*-stem is often considered a subclass of the *iā*-stems. This means in practice that in all except four cases, the pattern for the *ī*-stems is *exactly* the same as that of the *iā*-stems. The four cases which have a form that does not correspond with the forms of the *iā*-stems are the nominative singular, the vocative singular, the nominative dual and the accusative dual (and if we would have a vocative dual, that would have looked like the nominative dual - so that would have been the fifth case that does not correspond with the pattern of *iā*-stems). Luckily, these four forms all look the same, so you won't have to learn loads of different forms! As you might expect, the mutation pattern is also exactly the same.

All words that belong to the *ī*-stem end in a **palatal or slender consonant (group)** and they usually consist of more than one syllable. Some examples of the words belonging to this stem: *inis* 'island', *séitig* 'wife, consort', *rígain* 'queen', *blíadain* 'year', *Brigit*. Keep in mind that when you add an ending to words that already have two syllables, you often get syncope.

You probably already know this, but I will mention it anyway as it is important to remember: personal names in Old Irish, such as Conn, Cú Chulainn, Brigit etc. are *declined* (i.e. they can take different cases, so you will find them in the nominative, dative, accusative, genitive and vocative, for example: *tech Cuinn*, 'Conn's house', *Ad-cí in fer Brigti*, 'the man sees Brigit' etc.).

And now the pattern for the *ī*-stems:.

31

Singular

Case	Form	Mutation	How to Reconstruct	Translation
Nom.	*rígain*	lenites	-----	queen
	inis			island
Voc.	*a rígain*	lenites	looks like nom.sg.	o, queen
	a inis			o, island
Acc.	*rígnai*	nasalizes	add the ending *-i*	queen
	insi			island
Gen.	*rígnae*	h-mutation	add the ending *-e*	of a queen
	inse			of an island
Dat.	*do rígnai*	lenites	add the ending *-i*	for a queen
	i n-insi			on an island

Plural

Case	Form	Mutation	How to Reconstruct	Translation
Nom.	*rígnai*	h-mutation	add the ending *-i*	queens
	insi			islands
Voc.	*a rígnai*	h-mutation	add the ending *-i*	o, queens
	a insi			o, islands
Acc.	*rígnai*	h-mutation	add the ending *-i*	queens
	insi			islands
Gen.	*rígnae*	nasalizes	add the ending *–e*	of queens,
	inse			of islands
Dat.	*do rígnaib*	none	add the ending *-(a)ib*	for queens
	i n-insib			on islands

Dual

Case	Form	Mutation	How to Reconstruct	Translation
Nom.	*dí rígain*	lenites	form looks like nom. sg.	two queens
	dí inis			two islands
Acc.	*dí rígain*	lenites	form looks like nom. sg.	two queens
	dí inis			two islands
Gen.	*dá rígnae*	lenites	add ending *-e*	of two queens
	dá inse			of two islands
Dat.	*do dib rígnaib*	none	add ending *-(a)ib*	for two queens
	do dib n-insib			for two islands

II.a.6. *i*-stems

(*GOI*: §§299-304; Lehmann: 19-20, 100; McCone: 23-6; Quin lesson 8; Stifter: 97-8; Strachan: 6-7; Tigges: 34)

i-stems can be masculine, feminine or neuter, though there are not that many neuter *i*-stems. The nominative singular ends in a **palatal consonant**. The only case that looks different from what we have seen so far is the genitive singular, which ends in the letter *-o* or *-a*. For those of you that are interested: the ending in -o is older than the ending in -a. Please note that if you have a noun that consists of neutral consonant (group) + vowel a + i-glide + palatal consonant (group), like *fraig*, 'wall', *daig*, 'fire, flame' *aig*, 'ice' and *tailm* 'sling', the -ai- changes to -e- when an ending is added, so in the genitive singular (*frego, dego, ego, telmo*), the plural (*fregai, degai, egai, telmai* etc.) and genitive and dative dual. Look also at the word *muir*, in which —ui- becomes -o- in the genitive singular.

i-stems masculine

Singular

Case	Form	Mutation	How to Reconstruct	Translation
Nom.	*liaig*	none	---	physician
Voc.	*a liaig*	none	form looks like nom.sg.	o, physician
Acc.	*liaig*	nasalizes	form looks like nom.sg.	physician
Gen.	*lego*	h-mut.	last consonant is made neutral, ending -o or —a added	of a physician
Dat.	*do liaig*	lenites	form looks like nom.sg.	for a physician

Plural

Case	Form	Mutation	How to Reconstruct	Translation
Nom.	*legai*	h-mut.	ending -(a)i is added	physicians
Voc.	*a legai*	h-mut.	form looks like nom.pl.	o, physicians
Acc.	*legai*	h-mut.	form looks like nom.pl.	physicians
Gen.	*legae*	nasalizes	ending -(a)e is added	of physicians
Dat.	*do legaib*	none	ending —(a)ib is added	for physicians

Dual

Case	Form	Mutation	How to Reconstruct	Translation
Nom.	*dá liaig*	lenites	form looks like nom.sg.	two physicians
Acc.	*dá liaig*	lenites	form looks like nom.sg.	two physicians
Gen.	*dá lego*	lenites	form looks like gen.sg.	of two physicians
Dat.	*do dib legaib*	none	ending —(a)ib is added	for two physicians

i-stems feminine

Singular

Case	Form	Mutation	How to Reconstruct	Translation
Nom.	*láir*	lenites	---	a mare
Voc.	*a láir*	lenites	form looks like nom.sg.	o, mare
Acc.	*láir*	nasalizes	form looks like nom.sg.	a mare
Gen.	*láro*	h-mut.	last consonant is made neutral, ending -o or —a	of a mare

Case	Form	Mutation	How to Reconstruct	Translation
			added	
Dat.	*do láir*	lenites	form looks like nom.sg.	for a mare

Plural

Case	Form	Mutation	How to Reconstruct	Translation
Nom.	*láiri*	h-mut.	ending -(*a*)*i* is added	mares
Voc.	*a láiri*	h-mut.	form looks like nom.pl.	o mares
Acc.	*láiri*	h-mut.	form looks like nom.pl.	mares
Gen.	*láire*	nasalizes	ending -(*a*)*e* is added	of mares
Dat.	*do láirib*	none	ending —(*a*)*ib* is added	for mares

Dual

Case	Form	Mutation	How to Reconstruct	Translation
Nom.	*dí láir*	lenites	form looks like nom.sg.	two mares
Acc.	*dí lair*	lenites	form looks like nom.sg.	two mares
Gen.	*dá láro*	lenites	form looks like gen.sg.	of two mares
Dat.	*do dib láirib*	none	ending —(*a*)*ib* is added	for two mares

i-stems neuter

Singular

Case	Form	Mutation	How to Reconstruct	Translation
Nom.	*muir*	nasalizes	---	sea
Voc.	*a muir*	nasalizes	form looks like nom.sg.	o sea
Acc.	*muir*	nasalizes	form looks like nom.sg.	sea
Gen.	*moro*	h-mut.	final consonant group made neutral; ending -*o* or -*a* added	of a sea
Dat.	*i muir*	lenites	form looks like nom.sg.	in a sea

Plural

Case	Form	Mutation	How to Reconstruct	Translation
Nom.	*Muire*	lenites	ending -*e* is added	seas
Voc.	*a muire*	lenites	form looks like nom.pl.	o, seas
Acc.	*muire*	lenites	form looks like nom.pl.	seas
Gen.	*muire*	nasalizes	form looks like nom.pl.	of seas
Dat.	*i muirib*	none	ending —(*a*)*ib* is added	in seas

Dual

Case	Form	Mutation	How to Reconstruct	Translation
Nom.	*dá muir*	nasalizes	form looks like nom.sg.	two seas
Acc.	*dá muir*	nasalizes	form looks like nom.sg.	two seas
Gen.	*dá moro*	nasalizes	form looks like gen.sg.	of two seas
Dat.	*i ndib muirib*	none	ending —(*a*)*ib* is added	in two seas

That is the whole pattern for *i*-stems. Not too difficult, now is it? Let us get on with the *u*-stems.

II.a.7. *u*-stems

(*GOI*: §§305-14; Lehmann: 19-20, 100; McCone: 23-6; Quin lesson 9; Stifter: 112-3; Strachan: 8; Tigges: 34)

In Old Irish, *u*-stems can be either masculine or neuter - although there are some feminine nouns that by Old Irish were declined like *ā*-stems that originally were considered *u*-stems, like *mucc*, 'pig' - but never mind that. Some things to note before I give you the paradigm:

(1) The nominative, vocative, accusative and dative singular end in a **neutral consonant**.

(2) The genitive singular has the ending *-o* or *-a* again, like the *i*-stems do.

(3) The nominative/vocative plural of masculine *u*-stems have three possible endings: *-a*, *-ai* or *-ae* (I am not going to discuss why; the oldest ending, according to Thurneysen, is the ending *-ae* - if you are very interested in this, you can look up §312 in his *Grammar of Old Irish*).

(4) The accusative plural of masculine *u*-stems ends in *-u*, like we have encountered in *o*-stems.

(5) The nominative/vocative/accusative plural of neuter *u*-stems can come in a short form or a longer form. As we have seen with *o*-stems, the longer form, ending in *-a*, is used to avoid confusion about whether a noun is singular or plural. The shorter form, which looks the same as the nominative/vocative/accusative singular, causes lenition.

(6) Note that sometimes vowel changes occur, for example changes from *-u-* to *-o-* and *-i-* to *-e-* in the genitive singular and in the plural!

And now for the paradigm!

u-stems masculine

Singular

Case	Form	Mutation	How to Reconstruct	Translation
Nom.	*guth*	none	----------------	voice
Voc.	*a guth*	none	form looks like nom.sg.	o voice
Acc.	*guth*	nasalizes	form looks like nom.sg.	voice
Gen.	*gotho*	h-mutation	ending *-o* or *-a* is added	of a voice
Dat.	*do guth*	lenites	form looks like nom.sg.	for a voice

Plural

Case	Form	Mutation	How to Reconstruct	Translation
Nom.	*gotha , gothae, gothai*	h-mutation	ending *–a, -ae* or *–ai* is added	voices
Voc.	*a gotha, a gothae, a gothai*	h-mutation	ending *-ae, -a* or *-ai* is added	o voices
Acc.	*guthu*	h-mutation	ending *-u* is added	voices
Gen.	*gothae*	nasalizes	ending *-(a)e* is added	of voices
Dat.	*do gothaib*	none	ending *–(a)ib* is added	for voices

Dual

Case	Form	Mutation	How to Reconstruct	Translation
Nom.	*dá guth*	lenites	form looks like nom.sg.	two voices
Acc.	*dá guth*	lenites	form looks like nom.sg.	two voices
Gen.	*dá gotho*	lenites	form looks like gen.sg.	of two voices
Dat.	*do dib ngothaib*	none	ending *–(a)ib* is added	for two voices

u-stems neuter

Singular

Case	Form	Mutation	How to Reconstruct	Translation
Nom.	*dorus*	nasalizes	---	a door
Voc.	*a dorus*	nasalizes	form looks like nom.sg.	o door
Acc.	*dorus*	nasalizes	form looks like nom.sg.	a door
Gen.	*doirseo*	h-mutation	ending *-o* or *-a* is added	of a door
Dat.	*for dorus*	lenites	form looks like nom.sg.	on a door

Note the genitive - the palatalization there is caused by syncope.

Plural

Case	Form	Mutation	How to Reconstruct	Translation
Nom.	*dorus*	lenites	form looks like nom.sg.	doors
	doirsea	h-mutation	ending *-a* is added	doors
Voc.	*a dorus*	lenites	form looks like nom.sg.	o doors
	a doirsea	h-mutation	ending *-a* is added	o doors
Acc.	*dorus*	lenites	form looks like nom.sg.	doors
	doirsea	h-mutation	ending *-a* is added	doors
Gen.	*doirse*	nasalizes	ending *-(a)e* is added	of doors
Dat.	*for doirsib*	none	ending *–(a)ib* is added	on doors

Note: the forms that look like nom. sg. lenite the following word if possible; the endings in *–a* do not! Compare this with the pattern for the o-stems neuter pleural.

Dual

Case	Form	Mutation	How to Reconstruct	Translation
Nom.	*dá dorus*	nasalizes	form looks like nom.sg.	two doors
Acc.	*dá dorus*	nasalizes	form looks like nom.sg.	two doors
Gen.	*dá doirseo*	h-mutation	form looks like gen.sg.	of two doors
Dat.	*for dib ndoirsib*	none	ending –(*a*)*ib* is added	on two doors

And that is the basic pattern for the *u*-stems, and the end of the discussion of the vocalic stems!

II.b. Consonantal stems

And now it is time for… the consonantal stems! As you are aware, all of the noun stem classes that we have seen up to now were vocalic stems (i.e. stems containing a vowel: *ā, o, io, iā, i, ī* and *u*-stems). As the name 'consonantal stem' suggests, we shall see that except for the nominative singular and sometimes the dative singular, the nouns will generally contain a certain consonant (the stem class determines what consonant this is, so an *n*-stem noun will contain the letter *n* where applicable).

There are five consonantal stems: guttural stems, dental stems, *n*-stems, *r*-stems and *s*-stems. Luckily for us, all of the masculine and feminine words of the consonantal stems follow one basic pattern regarding endings and mutations (lenition etc.) – which is why I can conveniently treat all of them in one fell swoop! The neuter consonantal stems also follow certain patterns, but they differ slightly from the masculine/feminine pattern. I will discuss them later. Please note that there *are* exceptions to the basic pattern, but you will find out about them under the discussions of the specific stem classes.

II.b.1. Basic pattern masculine/feminine consontantal stems

First, let me give you the basic pattern for the **masculine** and the **feminine** words:

Singular

Nom.	for the nominative, there is no fixed rule – sorry, everyone!
Voc.	looks like the nominative singular
Acc.	ends in palatal consonant, causes nasalization
Gen.	ends in neutral consonant
Dat.	ends in palatal consonant, causes lenition. The dative sometimes has a special short form that looks like the nominative singular

Plural

Nom.   ends in palatal consonant

Voc.   looks like the accusative plural. Often you will find syncope.

Acc.   ends in neutral consonant + *a*, causes h-mutation. Often, you will find syncope.

Gen.   ends in neutral consonant, causes nasalization

Dat.   ends in a palatal *b*, added to the particular consonant of the stem class (so consonant + vowel + palatal *b*). Often, you will find syncope.

Dual

Note: the nominative and accusative dual sometimes use the same short form that we have seen in the dative singular – preceded by the numeral *dá*, of course.

Nom.   ends in palatal consonant.

Acc.   looks same as nominative dual

Gen.   ends in neutral consonant

Dat.   ends in consonant + vow'l + palatal *b*. Often, you will find syncope here.

Now that we have the basic pattern, let us go on to the different consonantal stem classes.

II.b.2. Guttural stems

(*GOI*: §§318-21; Lehmann: 27, 105; McCone: 24-6; Quin lesson 15; Stifter: 148-9; Strachan: 10; Tigges: 49-50)

Guttural stems (sometimes also called **velar stems**) are stems that end in a guttural consonant, that is to say, in *c* (sounds like *k*), *g* or *ch*. Try to pronounce these consonants. Can you feel them in the back of your throat? That is why they are called guttural stems! This guttural consonant (group) will appear **in all cases except for the nominative and vocative singular and sometimes the dative singular and nominative and accusative dual**.

A distinction is made between lenited and unlenited guttural stems. In lenited guttural stems, the guttural consonant (group) you will see is either *ch* or *g* (so lenited *c* or lenited *g*); there is one word that we know that is an unlenited guttural stem, *lië* 'stone' (I will discuss it below); there, the consonant you will see is *c*. In the *Dictionary of the Irish Language* (DIL from now on), lenited guttural stems are indicated by placing *g,m* or *g,f* after the noun (referring to guttural stem masculine and feminine respectively); *lië* is

38

indicated as *nk,m*.

Lenited guttural stems

The general rule about when you find *ch* and when you see *g* is that if the ending is palatal, you will usually find a (lenited) *g*; if it is neutral, *ch* is generally used. Let us look at the pattern for some of the guttural stems. The words used are *cathair*, a feminine guttural stem meaning 'city'; *nathair*, another feminine guttural stem meaning 'snake', *aire*, a masculine guttural stem meaning '(a) noble(man)', and finally *rí*, a masculine guttural stem meaning 'king'. Note that they follow the above pattern, and that there are no differences between the masculine and feminine patterns:

Singular

Nom.	*cathair, nathair, aire, rí*
Voc.	*a chathir, a nathir, a aire, a rí*
Acc.	*cathraig, nathraig, airig, ríg*
Gen.	*cathrach, nathrach, airech, ríg*
Dat.	*cathraig, nathraig, airig, ríg*
or	*caithir, naithir, aire, rí*

Plural

Nom.	*cathraig, nathraig, airig, ríg*
Voc.	*a chathracha, a nathracha, a airecha, a rega*
Acc.	*cathracha, nathracha, airecha, rega*
Gen.	*cathrach, nathrach, airech, ríg*
Dat.	*cathrachaib, nathrachaib, airechaib, rígaib*

Dual

Nom.	*dí chathraig, dí nathraig, dá airig, dá ríg* <u>or</u> *dí chathir, dí nathir, dá aire, dá rí*
Acc.	*dí chathraig, dí nathraig, dá airig, dá ríg* <u>or</u> *dí chathir, dí nathir, dá aire, dá rí*
Gen.	*dá chathrach, dá nathrach, dá airech, dá ríg*
Dat.	*dib catrachaib, dib natrachaib, dib n-airechaib, dib rígaib*

Did you notice that almost all cases contain or end in the guttural? Well done. Of course, since I emphasized the guttural, it is pretty hard to miss.

Unlenited guttural stems

There is one word, however, that is known as an *unlenited* guttural stem: the word *lïe*, a masculine hiatus word (in case you forgot what a hiatus word is: the two vowels that stand next to each other are pronounced separately, so something like l*i*-e). The pattern is exactly like the basic pattern described

39

above:

	Singular	**Plural**	**Dual**
Nom.	*lie*	*lieic*	*dá lieic*
Voc.	*a lie*	*a leca*	---
Acc.	*lieic*	*leca*	*dá lieic*
Gen.	*liac*	*liac*	*dá liac*
Dat.	*lieic*	*lecaib*	*dib lecaib*

See, it is not that hard at all. We are already done with the guttural stems. Let us now go on to the next group: dental stems.

II.b.3. Dental stems

(*GOI*: §§322-6; Lehmann: 27, 105; McCone: 24-6; Quin lessons 16,17; Stifter: 160-2; Strachan: 11-2; Tigges: 49-50)

Dental stems end where appropriate in a dental (duh). A dental consonant (group) is a consonant (group) that you pronounce with your teeth, i.e. '*d*', '*t*' or '*th*' (you can try it if you want to – or think of the word 'dentist'). As with the guttural stems, there are two kinds of dental stems: lenited and unlenited dental stems.

Lenited dental stems

Most of the nouns in the dental stem class are lenited dental stems, meaning that in most cases they contain either *th* or lenited *d*. In *DIL*, they are referred to as *d,m* or *d,f*, e.g.'*cré*, d,f'. Let's look at a few of them. I chose *eirr*, 'chariot-fighter', d,m; *traig*, 'foot', d,f, *gleo*, 'fight', d,f and *fili*, d,m 'poet'.

Singular

Nom.	*eirr, traig, gléo, fili*
Voc.	*a eirr, a thraig, a gléo, a fili*
Acc.	*eirrid, traigid, glieid, filid*
Gen.	*erred, traiged, gliad, filed*
Dat.	*eirrid, traigid, glieid, filid*

Plural

Nom.	*eirrid, traigid, glieid, filid*
Voc.	*a erreda, a traigthea, a gliada, a fileda*
Acc.	*erreda, traigthea, gliada, fileda*
Gen.	*erred, traiged, gliad, filed*
Dat.	*erredaib, traigthib, gliadaib, filedaib*

Dual

Nom.	*dá eirrid, dí thraigid, dí glieid, dá filid*
Acc.	*dá eirrid, dí thraigid, dí glieid, dá filid*
Gen.	*dá erred, dá traiged, dá gliad, dá filed*
Dat.	*dib n-erredaib, dib traigthib, dib ngliadaib, dib filedaib*

Unlenited dental stems

The unlenited dental stems (in *DIL* referred to as 't,m' etc., e.g. *carae*, t,m 'friend') have a little story behind them. All of the words in this stem class go back to words that used to end in **nt*, e.g. *dét*, 'tooth' (in English, you still have this *nt*-combination. Just think of the word *dental*). In Irish, they (originally) did not use the combination **nt*. Instead, they left out the letter *n*. This had two consequences:

(1) the word remained an *unlenited dental stem*.
(2) if the **nt* stood in stressed position, as is the case in the word *dét*, **compensatory lengthening** was used. Compensatory lengthening is the lengthening of a vowel to compensate for the loss of a following consonant. If this group stood in unstressed position, there was no compensatory lengthening, like in *carat*, 'of a friend', where you find *carat* instead of **carát*.

	Singular	Plural	Dual
Nom.	*námae*	*námait*	*dá námait*
Voc.	*a námae*	*a náimtea*	-----------
Acc.	*námait*	*náimtea*	*dá námait*
Gen.	*námat*	*námat*	*dá námat*
Dat.	*námait*	*náimtib*	*dá náimtib*

II.b.4. *n*-stems

(*GOI*: §§327-33; Lehmann: 36; McCone: 24-6; Quin lesson 18; Stifter: 209-10; Strachan: 13; Tigges: 49-50)

There is nothing abnormal about the masculine and feminine words in this stem class. They all follow the basic pattern discussed above. One thing that might strike you as odd if you look them up in (for example) Strachan's *Paradigms*, is the fact that the noun *brithem*, 'judge', has a genitive singular *brithemon*, and a dative and accusative singular *brithemain*. The letters *o* and *a* here represent the same sound. Because the last syllable was unstressed, the pronunciation became less clear, and vowels were pronounced as 'uh' (in texts on grammar referred to as /ə/ or 'schwa'). Because Irish did not have a letter for this sound, people were unsure of how to spell it, and used different vowels for it. This led to a lot of confusion with regard to endings in Middle Irish – but that is something for another day (and another book). Let us take a look at some of the nouns in this stem class: *cú*, a masculine *n*-stem meaning 'dog', and *an(a)im*, a feminine *n*-stem, meaning 'soul'.

	Singular	Plural	Dual
Nom.	*cú, anim*	*coin, anmain*	*dá choin, dí anmain*
Voc.	*a chú, a anim*	*a cona, a anmana*	----
Acc.	*coin, anmain*	*cona, anmana*	*dá choin, dí anmain*
Gen.	*con, anman*	*con, anman*	*dá chon, dá anman*
Dat.	*coin, anmain*	*conaib, anmanaib*	*dib conaib, dib n-anmanaib*

Unlenited *n*-stems (sometimes referred to as *MacNéill's Law*)

Unlenited *n*-stems, that have *–nn* in all of the places where the other *n*-stems just have one, are those words belonging to the *n*-stems with a nominative singular of which the second syllable starts in *r*, *l*, *n* or *mm* (almost always, words in this stem class end in the letter '*(i)u*'. This is sometimes called MacNéill's Law. You could simplify the rule for yourself by saying that you get MacNéill's Law (*-nn*) if the letter before the *-(i)u* is an *r*, *l*, *n* or *mm*). The pattern is the same as that of the *n*-stems.

Be careful: there is one word that takes *–nn* even though it does not have a second syllable beginning in *r*, *l*, *n* or *mm*: *gobae*, a masculine *n*-stem meaning 'smith' (gen. *gobann* etc.). Now, let's take a look at a few words in this group: *Ériu*, 'Ireland', n,f, *íriu*, n,f, 'land', and *Bricriu*, n,m 'Bricriu' – I am giving you the names *Ériu* and *Bricriu* in the singular only, because Bricriu is a personal name and there is only one Ireland.

	Singular	Plural	Dual
Nom.	*Ériu, íriu, Bricriu*	*írinn*	*dí írinn*
Voc.	*a Ériu, a íriu, a Bricriu*	*a írenna*	---
Acc.	*Érinn, írinn, Bricrinn*	*írenna*	*dí írinn*
Gen.	*Érenn, írenn, Bricrenn*	*írenn*	*dá írenn*
Dat.	*Érinn, írinn, Bricrinn*	*írennaib*	*dib n-írennaib*

II.b.5. *r*-stems
(*GOI*: §§334-6; Lehmann: 36, 111-2; McCone: 24-6; Quin lesson 20; Stifter: 175-6; Strachan: 15; Tigges: 49-50)

The *r*-stems are the *only* consonantal stems of which the nominative singular contains the consonant of the stem class they belong to (the *r*). The *r*-stems have one form that does not follow the general pattern, and that is the

genitive plural. Instead of ending in a neutral consonant, the genitive plural ends in the letter *–e*:

	Singular	Plural	Dual
Nom.	*athair, siur*	*aithir, sethir*	*dá athair, dí fiur*
Voc.	*a athair, a fiur*	*a athra, a sethra*	---
Acc.	*athair, sieir*	*athra, sethra*	*dá athair, dí fiur*
Gen.	*athar, sethar*	**aithre, seithre**	*dá athar, dá fethar*
Dat.	*athair, sieir* *dib sethraib*	*athraib, sethraib*	*dib n-athraib,*

The problem of *siur*

You have probably noticed a few abnormal things in the paradigm of *siur*. One of those is that with a few exceptions, all forms have *–th–* in the middle. This is in analogy with the other words in this stem class *athair*, *máthair* and *brathair* – they all have that *–th–*, so eventually it spread to the word *siur*. Another abnormal thing can be seen in the vocative singular and in the nominative and accusative dual. Instead of the expected **a śiur*, with a punctum delens over the *s*, we see *a fiur*. Let me explain. The *s–* in the word *siur* does not just stand for the letter *s–*. It stands for the sound '*sw*'. For those of you who have learned German, you still find it in the word for sister, 'Schwester'. When the word *siur* is lenited in Old Irish, the *s–* is replaced by the letter *f–*. There are only a few words in Irish that have this. *Sesser*, 'six men' is another one of these words. If you wish to say 'seven men', in Old Irish they say *mórfesser*, literally 'a big six of men'.

II.b.6. *s*-stems

(*GOI*: §§337-9; Lehmann: 27; McCone: 24-6; Quin lesson 21; Stifter: 176-7; Strachan: 16; Tigges: 49-50)

There is only one noun in the *s*-stem class that is a masculine word. All the other words in this stem class are neuter. The word in question is *mí*, 'month', and it follows our basic pattern:

	Singular	Plural	Dual
Nom.	*mí*	*mís*	*dá mís*
Voc.	*a mí*	*a mísa*	-------
Acc.	*mís*	*mísa*	*dá mís*
Gen.	*mís*	*mís*	*dá mís*
Dat.	*mís*	*mísaib*	*dib mísaib*

And there you have it! We are done with the masculine and feminine consonantal stems! Now, to help you see the pattern even better, I have made an overview with words from all the different consonantal stems masculine and feminine so you can compare them. Forms that deviate from the pattern are given in bold letters:

Singular

	g-stems	*d*-stems	*n*-stems	*r*-stems	*s*-stems
Nom.	*sail*	*arae*	*escung*	*máthair*	*mí*
Voc.	*a sail*	*a arae*	*a escung*	*a máthair*	*a mí*
Acc.	*sailig*	*araid*	*escongain*	*máthair*	*mís*
Gen.	*sailech*	*arad*	*escongan*	*máthar*	*mís*
Dat.	*sailig*	*araid*	*escongain*	*máthair*	*mís*

Plural

	g-stems	*d*-stems	*n*-stems	*r*-stems	*s*-stems
Nom.	*sailig*	*araid*	*escongain*	*máithir*	*mís*
Voc.	*a sailecha*	*a arada*	*a escongna*	*a máithrea*	*a mísa*
Acc.	*sailecha*	*arada*	*escongna*	*máithrea*	*mísa*
Gen.	*sailech*	*arad*	*escongan*	**máithre**	*mís*
Dat.	*sailechaib*	*aradaib*	*escongnaib*	*máithrib*	*mísaib*

Dual

	g-stems	*d*-stems	*n*-stems
Nom.	*dí sailig*	*dá araid*	*dí escongain*
Acc.	*dí sailig*	*dá araid*	*dí escongain*
Gen.	*dá sailech*	*dá arad*	*dá escongan*
Dat.	*dib sailechaib*	*dib aradaib*	*dib n-escongnaib*

	r-stems	*n*-stems
Nom.	*dí máithir*	*dá mís*
Acc.	*dí máithir*	*dá mís*
Gen.	*dá máthar*	*dá mís*
Dat.	*dib máithrib*	*dib mísaib*

II.b.7. Neuter consonantal stems

There are two basic patterns for the neuter consonantal stems. One of them is adopted by neuter dental stems, the other pattern is used by the neuter *n*-stems. The *s*-stems seem to use a combination of the two patterns. I will give you the basic pattern under each stem class.

II.b.8. Neuter dental stems

(*GOI*: §§315-26, esp. §325; Lehmann: 27, 105; McCone: 24-6; Quin lesson 17; Stifter: 162; Strachan: 12; Tigges: 49-50)

The pattern for neutral dental stems generally follows the pattern for masculine and feminine stems – with the usual exceptions of the vocative and accusative singular, accusative dual and the vocative and accusative plural, because, as you all well know by now, the vocative and accusative of neuter words look the same as the nominative. A difference with the masculine/feminine pattern: the **nominative plural** (and therefore the vocative and accusative plural) and the **nominative dual** (and therefore the accusative dual) of the neuter dental stems end in a **neutral consonant** instead of a palatal consonant. Also, remember that the nominative, vocative and accusative singular and the nominative and accusative dual cause **nasalization** of a following word, where possible. Here is an example:

	Singular	**Plural**	**Dual**
Nom.	*dét* (nasalizes)	*dét*	*dá ndét*
Voc.	*a dét* (nasalizes)	*a dét*	--------
Acc.	*dét* (nasalizes)	*dét*	*dá ndét*
Gen.	*dét*	*dét* (nasalizes)	*dá ndét*
Dat.	*déit* (lenites)	*détaib*	*dib ndétaib*

And that is what a neuter dental stem looks like!

Neuter *n*-stems

(*GOI*: §§327-33; Lehmann: 36; McCone: 24-6; Quin lesson 19; Stifter: 195-6; Strachan: 13-4; Tigges: 49-50)

The pattern that is used by neuter *n*-stems and, to an extent, by *s*-stems, has only two forms that look really different: the genitive singular and the dative singular. Let us take a look:

Basic Pattern:

Singular
Nom.	---------, causes nasalization
Voc.	Looks same as nominative singular, with of course the addition of the particle *a*; causes nasalization
Acc.	Looks same as nominative singular, causes nasalization
Gen.	Ends in –*e*, which is added to the nominative singular (this

often causes syncope). This means that you will not see the characteristic consonant of the stem class here (in this case the letter *n*).

Dat.   Ends in *–im*, which is added to the nominative singular (also often causes syncope). Again, you do not see the consonant of the stem class. Causes lenition.

Plural

Nom.   Like neuter dental stems, the nominative plural ends in a neutral consonant

Voc.   Looks like the nominative plural (don't forget the *a*!)

Acc.   Looks like the nominative plural

Gen.   Ends in neutral consonant and causes nasalization.

Dat.   Ends in palatal *–b*, which is added to the consonant (so again, consonant + vowel + palatal *b*)

Dual

Nom.   Looks like nominative singular, causes nasalization

Acc.   Looks like nominative dual, causes nasalization

Gen.   Ends in neutral vowel

Dat.   Ends in palatal *–b*, like the dative plural

Here are some examples. I used the nouns *béim*, 'blow' (as in 'a blow to the head') and *ainm*, 'name':

	Singular	Plural	Dual
Nom.	*béim, ainm*	*béimmen, anman*	*dá mbéim, dá n-ainm*
Voc.	*a béim, a ainm*	*a béimmen, a anman*	---
Acc.	*béim, ainm*	*béimmen, anman*	*dá mbéim, dá n-ainm*
Gen.	*béimme, anmae*	*béimmen, anman*	*dá mbéimmen, dá n-anman*
Dat.	*béimmim, anmaim*	*béimmenaib, anmanaib*	*dib mbéimmenaib dib n-anmanaib*

Neuter *s*-stems

(*GOI*: §§337-9; Lehmann: 27; McCone: 24-6; Quin lesson 21; Stifter: 176-7; Strachan: 16; Tigges: 49-50)

This brings us to the last consonant stem class – neuter *s*-stems This stem class does not have all that many nouns. There is only one problem: neuter *s*-stems do not have the letter 's' in *any* case. The only noun in the *s*-stems that does show an 's' is the one masculine s-stem that I have discussed above. So this is a little tricky – but not too difficult.

As for the pattern, it is reasonably straightforward:

The nominative, vocative and accusative singular all look the same. The genitive singular, as with the *n*-stems, ends in the letter –*e*. The dative singular ends in a palatal consonant (like we have seen with the neuter nouns of the dental stem). The nominative, vocative, accusative *and* genitive plural all end in the letter –*e* (and note that in those cases, the preceding consonant is made palatal). The dative plural, as always, ends in a palatal –*b*. The nominative and accusative dual look like the nominative singular, the genitive dual ends in –*e* (again, with palatal consonant preceding it) and the dative dual (surprise!) ends in a palatal –*b*.

The mutation pattern is the same as for the other neutral consonantal stems: nominative, vocative, accusative singular nasalize; dative singular lenites; genitive plural nasalizes, and nominative and accusative dual nasalize as well.

To make this more clear, I here give you some of the nouns of the neuter *s*-stems: *glenn*, 'valley', *mag*, 'field', and *síd*, 'elfmound'.

	Singular	Plural	Dual
Nom.	*glenn, mag, síd*	*glinne, maige, síde*	*dá nglenn, dá mag, dá síd*
Voc.	*a glenn, a mag, a síd*	*a glinne, a maige, a síde*	---
Acc.	*glenn, mag, síd*	*glinne, maige, síde*	*dá nglenn, dá mag, dá síd*
Gen.	*glinne, maige, síde*	*glinne, maige, síde*	*dá nglinne, dá maige, dá síde*
Dat.	*do glinn, do maig, do síd*	*do glinnib, do maigib, do sídib*	*do dib nglinnib, do dib maigib, do dib sídib*

And these are the basics of the consonantal stems, which means we have finished with the nouns. On to the adjective!

III. THE ADJECTIVE

As stated before, a noun describes a person ('man'), place ('house') or thing ('vase') - basically everything that you can put the article 'the' in front of. These nouns can be accompanied by adjectives. Adjectives are words that give you additional information about nouns. They can describe things like size, quantity, color and quality (a **big** house, a **small** dog, a **large** drink, a **yellow** dress, etc.). There are two ways in which an adjective can be used: it can be used (1) attributively and (2) predicatively.

The attributive adjective

This usage of the adjective is probably the more common of the two. An attributive adjective accompanies the noun. In English, attributive adjectives stand in front of the noun. Examples of attributive adjectives: the **big, ugly, slimy, silver** fish. In Irish, attributive adjectives usually **follow the noun** about which they give additional information, e.g. *int ech* **már** 'the big horse'.

The adjective has to have the same **gender, case** and **number** as the noun. So if you have a noun in the nominative plural feminine, the adjective that goes with the noun will also stand in the nominative plural feminine. However, there are no special dual forms of the adjective left in Old Irish, so if a noun is found in the dual, the plural form of the adjective is used. Of course, the adjective still has to correspond in **case** (nominative, vocative etc.) and **gender** (masculine, feminine, neuter) to the noun: in *in dá macc choím*, 'the two shapely boys', the adjective *choím* (which is lenited here because the nom. dual masc. of the *o*-stems lenites) stands in the nominative masculine plural.

The predicative adjective

The word predicate is often used in conjunction with the copula (one of the verbs used for 'to be' - see chapter IX). The predicate is that part of a sentence that gives **additional information about the subject** of that sentence (in the sentence 'John is handsome', 'handsome' is the predicate, giving information about the subject, 'John'). A predicate can be a noun, an adjective, a pronoun or an adverb(ial phrase). The adjective used in this sense, so as the predicate of the subject ('the house is **small**', 'the food is **tasty**'), is called a **predicative adjective**. In Old Irish, the predicative adjective usually stands **directly after the copula**. Again, the adjective has to correspond with the noun in case, gender and (when possible) number: *it* *bicc in chlaidib*, 'the swords are small', with both *bicc* 'small' and *chlaidib* 'swords' in nominative plural masculine; *is amrae a mbiad*, 'the food is wonderful', where *amrae* 'wonderful' and *mbiad* 'food' are both nominative singular neuter. Here is a small overview for clarity's sake:

adjective	used attributively	used predicatively
small	a small house	the house is small
becc	*tech mbecc*	*is becc a tech*
big	a big man	the man is big
már, mór	*fer már*	*is már in fer*

Adjectives prefixed to nouns or verbs
(*GOI*: §384; McCone: -; Quin: -; Stifter: 80; Strachan: - ; Tigges: 108-9)

There are a few adjectives that are really only used in combination with other words (that is to say, they don't occur independently). Usually, these other words are nouns, but they can also be other adjectives or verbs. In these instances, the adjective stands in front of the other word and is not declined (so it doesn't take any other form). When adjectives are prefixed to nouns, the noun is lenited, if possible, and when adjectives are combined with verbs, they tend to stand before the stress. Some of the more common adjectives that are prefixed to other words are are: *caín* 'fine, beautiful', *dag* 'good', also *mad* 'good' and *so* 'good', *do* 'bad', *droch* 'bad', *mí* 'bad, evil' *mos* 'soon', *ro* 'very'. Some examples with nouns: *sochenél* 'a good kindred', *dochenél* 'a bad kindred', *dagduine* 'good person'; an example with a verb: *madgénair* 'he/she was well born'.

The words *uile* 'every, all, whole' and *sain* 'separate' can stand before the noun without forming a compound with them. In this case, the adjectives do take endings, e.g. *int uile thúath*, 'the whole tribe'.

Adjective stems
Like nouns, adjectives come in different stem classes. Luckily for us, we are only dealing with three of them here: the *o,ā*-stems, the *io,iā*-stems and the *i*-stems. Although there are others, for example a class of *u*-stems (see for example Strachan's *Paradigms*: 20-1 and *GOI* §§358-9) and one example of an unlenited dental stem adjective (*tee*, 'warm', for which the nom. pl. *teit* has been attested), I am leaving those out, since they are extremely rare. The good news is that you already know almost all of the forms (that is, if you have learned the patterns for the nouns), so you will not have to learn many new ones.

49

III.a. *o,ā*-stems

(*GOI*: §§350-3; Lehmann: 43; McCone: 29; Quin lesson 24; Stifter: 53; Strachan: 17; Tigges: 21-3)

The *o,ā*-stems are called this for good reason. Adjectives of this stem class are declined **exactly** like the *o*-stem nouns if the adjective is masculine or neuter (i.e., masculine adjectives in this stem class follow the pattern of the nouns of the *o*-stem masculine, neuter adjectives that of the *o*-stem neuter) and exactly like an *ā*-stems if it is feminine; this includes the mutation pattern. There are two exceptions: in the masculine vocative and accusative plural cases, you also find an ending in *–a* (as I am sure you remember, the *o*-stems masculine have an accusative plural ending in *–u*, e.g. *firu* 'men'). This ending of the adjective in *–a* was originally found in the vocative and accusative plural feminine and neuter; it then spread to the forms in the masculine (so you can for example find either *inna firu biccu* or *inna firu becca* in texts), and the ending in *-a* ended up replacing the older ending in *–u*. This starts to happen in Old Irish already, which is why for example the *Paradigms* lists both forms. Like nouns of these stem classes, *o,ā*-stem adjectives have a nominative singular ending in a neutral consonant. Let us take a look at the forms – and feel free to compare the patterns of the adjectives with those of the nouns, just to make sure I am not making this up:

Singular

	Masculine	Feminine	Neuter
Nom.	*becc*	*becc* (lenites)	*becc* (nasalizes)
Voc.	*bicc* (lenites)	*becc* (lenites)	*becc* (nasalizes)
Acc.	*becc* (nasalizes)	*bicc* (nasalizes)	*becc* (nasalizes)
Gen.	*bicc* (lenites)	*bicce*	*bicc* (lenites)
Dat.	*biucc* (lenites)	*bicc* (lenites)	*biucc* (lenites)

Plural

	Masculine	Feminine	Neuter
Nom.	*bicc* (lenites)	*becca* (h-mutation)	*becca* (h-mutation)
Voc.	*biccu/ becca*	*becca* (h-mutation)	*becca* (h-mutation)
Acc.	*biccu/ becca*	*becca* (h-mutation)	*becca* (h-mutation)
Gen	*becc* (nasalizes)	*becc* (nasalizes)	*becc* (nasalizes)
Dat.	*beccaib*	*beccaib*	*beccaib*

III.b. *io,iā*-stems

(*GOI*: §§354-5; Lehmann: pattern not given; McCone: 29; Quin lesson 27; Stifter: 76, 84; Strachan: 18; Tigges: 21-3)

As you might have expected, *io,iā*-stems are declined like *io*-stem nouns in the masculine and neuter forms and as an *iā*-stem in the feminine forms. Like nouns of this stem class, *io,iā*-adjectives are polysyllabic and have a nominative singular ending in the letter −*e*. Note that in the masculine vocative and accusative plural there is no form in −*u*: that has been assimilated to the feminine and neuter forms (compare this with the accusative plural masculine of the *o,ā*-stem adjectives above, where a similar development takes place):

Singular

	Masculine	Feminine	Neuter
Nom.	*buide*	*buide* (lenites)	*buide* (nasalizes)
Voc.	*buidi* (lenites)	*buide*	*buide* (nasalizes)
Acc.	*buide* (nasalizes)	*buidi* (nasalizes)	*buide* (nasalizes)
Gen.	*buidi* (lenites)	*buide*	*buidi* (lenites)
Dat.	*buidiu* (lenites)	*buidi* (lenites)	*buidiu* (lenites)

Plural

	Masculine	Feminine	Neuter
Nom.	*buidi* (lenites)	*buidi*	*buidi*
Voc.	*buidi*	*buidi*	*buidi*
Acc.	*buidi*	*buidi*	*buidi*
Gen.	*buide* (nasalizes)	*buide* (nasalizes)	*buide* (nasalizes)
Dat.	*buidib*	*buidib*	*buidib*

III.c. *i*-stems

(*GOI*: §§356-7; Lehmann: pattern not given; McCone: 29; Quin lesson 28; Stifter: 99; Strachan: 19; Tigges: 21-3)

It is getting very predictable at this point: adjectives belonging to the *i*-stems are mostly declined like nouns in the *i*-stem; likewise, the nominative singular of adjectives of this stem class ends in a palatal consonant. There are three things that are different from the pattern of *i*-stem nouns: first of all, the **genitive singular**, which in nouns of this stem class ends in −*o* or −*a* (*liaig*, gen.sg. *lego* etc.) has been simplified for adjectives in the *i*-stems and looks like genitive singular of *o*-stems (ending in a palatal consonant) and *ā*-stems (ending in −*e*). Second of all, the **nominative, vocative and accusative plural neuter**: for nouns this ends in −*e*, for adjectives (in

51

analogy with the masculine and feminine adjectives) they end in *–i*. Finally, the **genitive plural**, which originally ended in *–e*, starts to lose that *–e*, in analogy with the adjectives of the other two stems.

Singular

	Masculine	**Feminine**	**Neuter**
Nom.	*maith*	*maith* (lenites)	*maith* (nasalizes)
Voc.	*maith*	*maith*	*maith* (nasalizes)
Acc.	*maith* (nasalizes)	*maith* (nasalizes)	*maith* (nasalizes)
Gen.	*maith*	*maithe*	*maith*
Dat.	*maith* (lenites)	*maith* (lenites)	*maith* (lenites)

Plural

	Masculine	**Feminine**	**Neuter**
Nom.	*maithi*	*maithi*	*maithi*
Voc.	*maithi*	*maithi*	*maithi*
Acc.	*maithi*	*maithi*	*maithi*
Gen.	*maith(e)* (nasalizes)	*maith(e)* (nasalizes)	*maith(e)* (nasalizes)
Dat.	*maithib*	*maithib*	*maithib*

One very important point:

> The adjective has to agree with the noun in **number, case and gender**. However, IT DOES NOT HAVE TO AGREE IN STEM CLASS.

In other words: you can get a noun in one stem (say an *n*-stem, like the word *cú* 'dog'), followed by an adjective in another stem (say an *o,ā*-stem like *cóem*), like *mét in chon bicc* 'the size of the small dog'. Because *cú* is a masculine word in the genitive singular, *bicc* is also a masculine word in the genitive singular. This has implications for mutations; while a noun from a certain stem, case and person may not cause a mutation, the adjective which comes form a different stem might, or vice versa. In this case, *chon* (gen. sg. of *n*-stem) doesn't lenite, but *bicc* (*o,ā*-stem adjective, gen. sg. masc.) would lenite a following word (for example a following preposition).

Two more examples of this:
In lebor maith 'the good book' – in this sentence, the noun is a masculine *o*-stem (*o,m*) and the adjective *i, m*.
Cú in brithemon maith 'the dog of the good judge' - the nouns are *n*-stems but the adjective is an *i*-stem.

And we are done with the patterns for the adjectival stems!

III.d. Degrees of comparison

At this stage, we have seen the different stem classes of the adjectives. But this does not mean we have come to the end of this chapter, because we still have to tackle something called the **degrees of comparison**. That might sound complicated, but it actually isn't really all that difficult. Degrees of comparison are used when you compare things (who would have guessed?): I am **as tall as** you, her eyes are **bluer than** his, Bill Gates used to be **the richest man** on the planet, etc.

The qualifiers used in these comparisons, 'tall', 'bluer', 'richest' are formed from adjectives (here 'tall', 'blue' and 'rich'), so the different degrees of comparison are ALWAYS made with adjectives. In Old Irish, there are three degrees of comparison:

(1) the **equative** degree,
(2) the **comparative** degree, and
(3) the **superlative** degree.

Let us take a look at each of those in turn.

III.d.1. The equative degree
(*GOI*: §§366, 368, 372, 376; Lehmann: 51; McCone: 32-3; Quin lesson 29; Stifter: 197-8; Strachan: 22-3; Tigges: 89-90)

The equative degree is used if you want to express that something is equal to something else. In English, this is expressed by the formula '*as X as Y*': my coat is *as warm as your coat*, that house is *as expensive as Buckingham Palace*, I am *as intelligent as you are*, etc.

In Old Irish, you can put an adjective in the equative degree by adding – *(a)ithir* or –*(a)idir*. Beware of vowel changes! The first ending is normally used after adjectives consisting of one syllable in their usual form, like *dían*, 'swift', which becomes *déinither*, 'as swift as' (with change of the diphthong *ía* > *é*). The second ending is often used after adjectives consisting of more than one syllable.

The *equative* degree **cannot be declined** (i.e. is not found in different forms) and is used predicatively with the copula (if you have forgotten what 'predicatively' means, see above under the predicative adjective). The object with which it is compared (so the Y in the formula *as X as Y*) stands in the **accusative case**.

To give you a couple of examples (I am giving you one in the singular and one in the plural to show you that the form doesn't change):

Is déinithir coin int ech	'the horse is as swift as a hound'
	(lit. 'it is as swift as a hound, the horse')
It déinithir cona ind eich	'the horses are as swift as hounds'

Let's move on to the next degree: the comparative!

III.d.2. The comparative degree
(*GOI*: §§366-7, 369, 372, 374-5, 377-8; Lehmann: 51; McCone: 32-3; Quin lesson 30; Stifter: 227-9; Strachan: 22-3; Tigges: 89-90)

The comparative degree is used to express the formula '*more X / X-er than Y*': *taller than he* is, *prettier than this, higher than the clouds, more vulnerable than a newborn baby*, etc.

How do you formulate this in Old Irish? Basically, you add *–u* or *–(i)u* to the normal nominative singular form of the adjective. Note that this sometimes causes vowel changes:

Adjective	+ Ending	= Comparative	
dían 'swift'	+ -*(i)u*	*déiniu*	'swifter'
ard 'high'	+ -*(i)u*	*ardu*	'higher'
ansae 'difficult'	+ -*(i)u*	*ansu*	'more difficult'
tromm 'heavy'	+ -*(i)u*	*trummu*	'heavier'

The comparative degree, like the equative, is used predicatively with the copula. It is also indeclinable, like the equative.

Now, how do you express the object of the comparison? There are two things you can do if you are dealing with a comparative degree:

(1) You use a noun in the **dative**, e.g. *is maissiu maínib*, 'it is more beautiful than treasures'. In this case, the dative is not preceded by a preposition;

(2) You use a form *ol-* or *in-* (originally a preposition) combined with forms of the substantive verb (*at-tá*, another form of the verb 'to be', see chapter IX.b.). Note that in all cases, the letter '*t*' that you might expect with the substantive verb has become a '*d*'). There are no forms attested for the first

and second persons plural in Old Irish, so I shall leave those out here:

	Subst. Verb	Object of comparison	Example
Sg. 1.	*at-tó* 'I am'	*oldó* 'than I am'	*siniu oldó* 'older than I am'
2.	*at-taí* 'you are'	*oldaí* 'than you are' *indaí*	*siniu indaí* 'older than you are'
3.	*at-tá* '(s)he/it is'	*oldaas* 'than (s)he/it is'	*trummu oldaas* 'heavier than he is'
Pl. 3.	*at-taat* 'they are' *indate*	*oldate* 'than they are'	*lobru oldate* 'weaker than they are'

For those of you who may be wondering what those strange-looking forms in the 3 sg. (ending in –*s*) and 3 pl. (ending in –*te*) are exactly (good question!) – they are relative forms of the (substantive) verb. If you have not yet encountered these, do not fret; all you have to do for the moment is recognize the forms. You will get to the relative at some stage, and then when you look at this again, it should all be clear.

Now, what do you do if the object of comparison (the Y in *X-er than Y*) is not a personal pronoun like 'me' or 'you', but a noun? Well, if you want to use a singular form of a noun, you put it after the *oldaas/indaas* form; if you need to use a noun in the dual or plural, you use *oldate/indate*.

> Look out: if a noun is used in combination with *oldaas/indaas* or *oldate/indate*, you put that noun in the **nominative case.**

An example: *is déniu int ech oldaas in cú*, 'the horse is swifter than the dog'

Let's look at the two possibilities of expressing the comparative in an example. If you want to say 'the companions are stronger than boys' (yes, I know, a weird sentence at best), you can do it by either putting the object of comparison ('boys' in our case) in the **dative**:

It tressa * **maccaib** *in chéili*
* *Tressa* is the irregular comparative form of *trén*, 'strong'

Alternatively, you can use a form of *ol-* or *in-* + substantive verb, followed by the noun **in the nominative.** Here the form we need is *oldate*, because the object of comparison is a noun in the plural:

It tressa in chéili oldate **maicc**

As you can see, it is really not that difficult. In fact, I think so highly of you that I believe we can safely move on to the last degree of comparison: the *superlative*.

III.d.3. The superlative degree

(*GOI*: §§366, 370-4; Lehmann: 51; McCone: 32-3; Quin lesson 31; Stifter: 211-2; Strachan: 22-3; Tigges: 89-90)

The superlative degree is used to express *'the X-est, the most X'*, as in *the best warrior, the highest mountain, the most annoying teacher*. In Old Irish, in order to put an adjective in the superlative, you add the ending *–am* or *–em* to the adjective (bear in mind that you can get syncope):

Adjective	Superlative Ending	Superlative Form
cóem 'shapely'	*-em*	*cóem**em*** 'shapeliest'
úasal 'noble'	*-em*	*úais**lem*** 'noblest'

Even in the irregular adjectives (see also below), the ending *–am/-em* is found in almost all instances, for example:

Adjective	Superlative Form
trén 'strong'	*tress**am*** 'strongest'
olc 'bad'	*mess**am*** 'worst'
már 'big, great'	*mo**am*** 'greatest'

Like the equative and comparative, the superlative is indeclinable. It is used predicatively with the copula: *in lóech **as moam*** 'the greatest warrior' (literally 'the warrior who is greatest', *inna ingena **ata tressam*** 'the strongest girls' (literally 'the girls who are strongest'). If additional information is given, that qualifies the superlative (e.g. 'the greatest **warrior of Ireland**'), this is expressed by using:

(1) the genitive: *is é as úaislem **lóech n-Érenn*** literally 'it is he who is noblest of the warriors of Ireland': 'he is the noblest of the warriors of Ireland' (you can see that *lóech* is genitive plural here because *Érenn* is nasalized), or:

(2) the preposition *di*: *is é as úaislem **di lóechaib Érenn***, 'he is the noblest of the warriors in Ireland'

And voilà – you have mastered the degrees of comparison! Well done. Here is a handy overview of what I just discussed, using *ard*, o,ā, 'high', in case you want to look this up quickly at a later stage:

positive:	*ard*		'high'
equative:	*aird**ithir*** + accusative		'as high as x'
comparative:	*ard**u*** + dative *or*		'higher than x'
	*ard**u*** + form of *ol-/in-*+		
	substantive verb + nominative		
superlative:	*ard**am*** (+ genitive/*di*)		'the highest'

III.d.4. Irregular forms

(*GOI*: §§372-3; Lehmann: 51; McCone: 32; Quin: -; Stifter 198, 212, 228; Strachan: 23; Tigges: 89)

Of course, there are some adjectives that form exceptions to these rules, and that have divergent forms in the degrees of comparison, like *il*, 'many, numerous', *lethan*, 'broad', *már/mór*, 'big', *oac*, 'young', *sír*, 'long', *trén*, 'strong', *remor*, 'fat', *accus/ocus*, 'near', *bec(c)*, 'small', *maith*, 'good', and *olc*, 'bad'. Of course, as is always the case, most of these words occur very frequently, so if you get the chance, learn them by heart! Trust me, it will come in handy. Here is an overview of the irregular forms found for these words:

Positve (=normal form)		Equative	Comparative	Superlative
accus,occus	'near'		*nessa*	*nessam*
becc	'small'		*lugu, laigiu, laugu*	*lugam, lugimem*
il	'many'	*lir*	*lia*	
lethan	'broad'	*leithir, leithidir, leithithir*	*letha*	
maith	'good'		*ferr*	*dech, deg*
már, mór	'great'	*máir, móir*	*mó, má, móo, móa, máo, móu, máa, maa, moo*	*máam, mám, moam*
oäc,[18] *óc*	'young'		*óä*	*óäm*
olc	'bad'		*messa*	*messam*
remor	'fat'	*reimir, reimithir*	*reime*	
sír	'long'	*sithir, sithithir*	*siä, sía*	*síam*
trén	'strong'	*treisithir*	*tressa*	*tressam*

---

[18] The umlaut indicates that this is a hiatus word (i.e. the vowels are pronounced separately).

III.e. Formation of adverbs

(*GOI*: 379-84; Lehmann: 71-2; McCone: - Quin: -; Stifter: - ; Strachan: -; Tigges:)

There are a number of ways in which you can turn an adjective into an adverb:

(1) The most common way to make an adverb is to use the preposition *co* 'up to' followed by the **neuter accusative singular** of the adjective, e.g. *co mór* 'greatly', *co maith* 'well', *co becc* 'little'.

(2) Another option is to use the **dat. sg. of the adjective**, preceded by what looks like the article, e.g. *in mór* 'greatly', *in maith* 'well', *in biucc* 'little'.
Sometimes, especially in legal texts, the article is omitted (so you may for example just find *biucc* rather than *in biucc*)

III.f. Adverbs of place

(*GOI*: §483; Lehmann: 71-2; McCone: - Quin: -; Stifter: - ; Strachan: -; Tigges: 112)

This section is perhaps somewhat out of place, but it is an important one, and I couldn't find a better location for it, so I apologize. There are a number of adverbs of place that are created from other adverbs or adjectives and can express **location**, i.e. a place where someone/something is; **departure**, i.e. where someone/something is going; and **place of origin**, i.e. from where someone/something is coming. Depending on what you want to express, you add a prefix to the basic form of the adverb or adjective (see below). The basic rule is the following: if you want to express a **location**, you prefix the letter *t*; if you want to express **departure**, you prefix the letter *s*; if you want to express a **place of origin**, you prefix *an*.

basic form	translation	location ('in the')	departure ('to the')	origin ('from the')
úas	above	*túas*	*súas*	*anúas*
ís	below	*tís*	*sís*	*anís*
air	in front/east	*tair*	*sair*	*anair*
íar	behind/west	*tíar*	*síar*	*aníar*
echta(i)r	outside	-	*sechta(i)r*	*anechta(i)r*

There are some adverbs that don't (entirely) follow this pattern. The word *sund* is especially abnormal:

basic form	translation	location	departure	origin
des(s)	south	*dess*	*fadess/sadess*	*andess*
túaid	north	*túaid*	*fa-thúaith/ sa-thúaith*	*a(n)túaid*
sund	here	*sund*	*ille*	*desíu*
all	there/beyond	*tall*	*innonn/innunn*	*anall*

IV. NUMERALS

There are two kinds of numbers: **cardinals**, these are your standard numbers 1, 2, 3, 54671, 28 etc, expressing an amount (think of Irish law texts that have sentences like 'How many kinds of king are there? Not difficult: seven kinds'); then there are the **ordinals**, meaning numbers like: first, third, fifteenth, hundredth, fourth and so on. You use *ordinals* when you are talking about a specific thing or person, as in 'the fourth person to finish the race'.

IV.a.Cardinals
(*GOI*: §§385-92; Lehmann: 43-4; McCone: 61-2; Quin: lesson 35; Stifter: 116-7, 163-4; Strachan: 23-4; Tigges: 72-3)

Cardinals usually precede the noun which they specify, like in English 'three women'. They can also stand on their own, in which case they are preceded by *a*, as is still the case in Modern Irish, as in Old Irish *a oín* (Mod. Ir. *a haon*) 'one', *a tri* (Mod. Ir. *a trí*) 'three'.

Only the numbers 2, 3, and 4 take different forms according to whether the following noun is masculine, feminine or neuter and according to the case of the noun (nominative, dative etc). All the other forms are uninflected, that is, they do not have any other forms. Let us first look at the numbers 1 – 10:

One
The Old Irish for 'one' is *oín-* or *óen-*. *Oín-* and *óen-* are always used in composition with the noun they qualify; that means that they are attached to the noun, and the initial of the noun is lenited, if possible. An example: *oínchenél*, 'one kindred, a single kindred', where the cardinal number *oín* is attached to the word *cenél* (the form *oín* is used here since the *c* in *cenél* is palatal). Since the initial of *cenél* can be lenited when the two words are combined, you get the resulting form *oínchenél* 'one race'. Often, simply a noun in the singular is used to express 'one' or 'a single', if there is not a lot of stress required. Obviously, the noun that the word *oín* and *óen* are attached to stands in the singular case.

Two

The number two, Old Irish *da* in masculine and neuter, or *di* in feminine, is followed by the noun in the **dual** and is **inflected**. You should be familiar with all of the forms of the number 2 already if you have read the section on the noun or the article, since these forms are used there in the dual cases! The pattern is as follows:

	masculine	feminine	neuter
Nom.	*da* (later *dá*), lenites	*di* (later *dí*), lenites	*da* (later *dá*), nasalizes
Acc.	*da* (later *dá*), lenites	*di* (later *dí*), lenites	*da* (later *dá*), nasalizes
Gen.	*da* (later *dá*), lenites	*da* (later *dá*), lenites	*da* (later *dá*), nasalizes
Dat.	*dib*, nasalizes	*dib*, nasalizes	*dib*, nasalizes

Three

All of the numbers from three onwards are followed by nouns in the **plural**. The Old Irish word for three is also inflected, and these are the forms you will find:

	masculine	feminine	neuter
Nom.	*tri*	*teoir/ teuir/ téora*	*tri*, lenites
Acc.	*tri*	*téora*	*tri*, lenites
Gen.	*tri*, nasalizes	*téora*, nasalizes	*tri*, nasalizes
Dat.	*trib*	*téoraib*	*trib*

Four

This is the only other cardinal that is inflected. These are the forms (* before a form means that that form has never actually been found in a text ('attested', to use a fancy word), and that it is reconstructed here):

	masculine	feminine	neuter
Nom.	*ceth(a)ir*	*cethéoir/ cethéora*	*ceth(a)ir*, lenites
Acc.	*cethri*	*cethéoir/ cethéora*	*ceth(a)ir*, lenites
Gen.	**cethre*, nasalizes	*cethéora*, nasalizes	**cethre*, nasalizes
Dat.	*cethrib*	*cethéoraib*	*cethrib*

Five

The Old Irish word for five is *coíc*, and it **lenites** the following noun when that stands in nom., acc., and dative plural, e.g. *ad-cíat coíc fir coíc maccu*, 'five men see five boys'. The word *coíc* **nasalizes** a noun in the genitive plural. *Coíc* is undeclined.

Six

The Old Irish for six is *sé*, and it causes **nasalization** if it stands before a **genitive plural**. In the other cases, it does nothing.

Seven, eight, nine and ten

Seven, Old Irish *secht*, eight, OI *ocht*, nine, OI *noí* and ten, OI *deich* all **nasalize** the following noun.

That wasn't all that hard, now was it? But what about the numbers up to twenty? And what of the multiples of ten? Well, I'm glad you ask:

11 – 19

The cardinals eleven through nineteen are expressed by adding *–deac* '-teen' (disyllabic, i.e. with two syllables, so a hiatus word, to brush up on your terminology) after the noun, and the rest of the number before the noun. A few examples: *tri fir deac*, 'thirteen men', *ocht n-eich deac*, 'eighteen horses', *di thuaith deac*, 'twelve tribes'. Note that the nouns are mutated based on the number that stands **in front** of it (so *tri*, *ocht* and *di* in the examples above).

Multiples of ten, up to 100

The multiples of ten are always considered to be substantives, and are followed by a noun in the **genitive plural** (so literally 'a thirty of trees' instead of 'thirty trees'). They are declined as a **unlenited dental stems masculine/feminine**. The forms are:

Twenty: *fiche*, gen. sg. *fichet*
Thirty: *tricho/tricha*, gen. sg. *trichot, trichat*
Fourty: *cethorcho*, gen. sg. *cethorchat*
Fifty: *coíca*, gen. sg. *coícat/cóecat*
Sixty: *sesca*, gen. sg. *sescot/sescat*
Seventy: *sechtmogo*, gen. sg. *sechtmogat*
Eighty: *ochtmoga*, gen. *ochtmugat*
Ninety: *nócha*, gen. *nóchat*

Hundred

The Old Irish for 'hundred' is *cét*, and it is declined as **an *o*-stem neuter**.

Thousand

The word for 'thousand' in Old Irish is *míle*, and it is a feminine ***iā*-stem**. If you wish to express 'a thousand warriors', this is usually done by putting the following noun in the genitive plural, *míle lóech*; but it can also be done by using the preposition *di* + dative (since *di* is followed by a dative case): *mile di lóechaib*.

61

Often, larger numbers are divided into smaller units, especially units of twenty and fifty, e.g. *tri coícait*, '150', literally 'three fifties', *secht fichit* '140' or 'seven score'. If one wishes to combine single digits and tens with hundreds (so 134, 753 etc.), you first give the single digit, then the tens, and you place the preposition *ar* before the hundred(s), so *tri fichet ar chét* '123'. If you would want to say '123 sons', you would place the noun after the single digit just like you do for the numbers 11-19; in this case the noun would come directly after the number 3: *tri maicc fichet ar chét*.

If you want to express really great numbers – *GOI* gives the number 185,000 in §391 – the process is very similar: basically, you give the first number (185 here) in the manner described above, adding the word for 'thousand', *míle* after the single digit; so 185,000 is *cóic míli ochtmugat ar chét*. Above I gave you the example of 123, *tri fichet ar chét* – if you wanted to change that to 123,000, you only need to add *míli* after *tri*: *tri míli fichet ar chét*.

IV.b. Ordinals
(*GOI*: §§393-8; Lehmann: 44; McCone: 63; Quin: lesson 35; Stifter 118, 164; Strachan: -; Tigges: 73)

Now, the other type of numeral, the **ordinal**. The ordinals behave like adjectives. They are found before the noun, except for the word for 'second', *tánaise*.

First
The word used for 'first' is *cétnae* (*io,iā*-stem); alternatively, you can make a compound by taking *cét-* and leniting the initial of the noun, where possible.

The word *cétnae* can also be used in the sense 'same', but in that meaning it ususally stands after the noun (so *in cétnae fer* 'the first man', *in fer cétnae* 'the same man').

Second
Tánaise (*io,iā* stem). This is the ONLY numeral which is found AFTER the noun that it qualifies, as in *in macc tánaise*, 'the second son'.

Third
Triss, tress. The ordinal *triss, tress* 'third' is uninflected.

Fourth, fifth, sixth, seventh, eighth, ninth, tenth, twentieth, thirtieth, hundredth:

4th:	*cethramad*
5th:	*cóiced*
6th:	*se(i)ssed*
7th:	*sechtmad*
8th:	*ochtmad*
9th:	*nómad*
10th:	*dechmad*
20th:	*fichetmad*
30th:	*trichatmad*
100th:	*cétmad*

All of these are inflected like *o,ā*-stem adjectives. For the numbers eleven through nineteen, *-deac* is added after the noun, in the same manner that you saw in the section on numerals, e.g. *in sechtmad fer deac*, 'the seventeenth man'. The only problem is the ordinal 'twelfth', because *tánaise*, as we have seen, is placed after the noun it qualified. The solution for this is to use a different word. The word used for 'twelfth' is *ala* combined with *deac*, as in *ala rann deac*, 'a twelfth part' or, combined with the article, *indala*, as in *indala n-ainm deac* 'the twelfth name'.

IV.c. Fractions
(*GOI*: §399; Lehmann: -; McCone:-; Quin: -; Stifter: 118, 164; Strachan: -; Tigges: -)

Something not often discussed in grammars, but useful to know, is what fractions and multiplicatives look like. These will be discussed in turn. First of all, **fractions**. If you wish to say 'half' ($1/2$), you simply use the word *leth* (o,n). This word can also be combined with the following noun; in that case, it stands in front of it (e.g., *lethrann*, 'half a stanza').

A third ($1/3$) is *trián* (a hiatus word – hence the umlaut). This word is neuter; the dative is *triun*.

A quarter ($1/4$) is *cethramthu*, a feminine *n*-stem, with gen. *cethramthan*. If you wish to express two quarters or three quarters, just use the cardinal number + *cethramthu*. The nominative plural is for example *téora cethramdin/*cethramthin*. Note that *cethramthu* is conjugated, and here, the form of the number three is as well, since that is one of the few numbers that have a distinctive feminine form as well as different forms in the different cases!

Starting with $^1/_5$, the neuter form of the ordinal is generally used substantivally (that is, it is not followed by a noun but stands on its own – alternatively, it can be followed by *rann* 'part'), e.g. *cóiced* 'a fifth', *cóic ochtmad* 'five eighths'.

IV.d. Multiplication

(*GOI*: §400; Lehmann: - ; McCone: -; Quin: -; Stifter: -; Strachan: -; Tigges: -)

This brings us to **multiplicatives**. If you want to say 'twice', 'three times', etc., you use the preposition *fo*, followed by the cardinal in the **accusative** case (unless of course the cardinal is indeclinable), e.g. *fo thri* 'three times', *fo fichit* 'twenty times'. If you wish to express '**x times y**', that is even simpler: in Irish, the order of the numbers is reversed, giving us '**y x**' – to put it differently: the second cardinal expresses how many times you need the first cardinal. That sounds a bit complicated, but it is actually pretty easy. Let me give you some examples:

tri secht means '7 x 3' (= '3, seven times' – if that helps); *cóic deich* '10 x 5 (5, ten times)'; *secht sescit* '60 x 7', and so on.

IV.e. One–ten persons, two – ten things

(*GOI*: §387, McCone: 62, Quin: -, Stifter: 231-2; Strachan: -; Tigges: 73)

Since this is something that you will find fairly often in texts, I thought I would discuss it very briefly here. If you wish to express 'one person, two persons, three persons' and so on, you generally use the appropriate cardinal and combine it with the word *fer* 'man' – which of course will be lenited, because that happens when you form compounds – the first letter of the second word is lenited, where possible. Note that in Old Irish, these words are conjugated as neuter *o*-stems (so dat. sg. *do oínur* 'for one person').

One - ten persons[19]

oínar, óenar	'1 person'
dïas	'2 persons'(this is obviously an exception as I am sure you have noticed): this is *á,f*, with gen. *deisse*, dat. and acc. *dïis*
triar	'3 persons'
cethrar	'4 persons'
cóicer	'5 persons'
se(i)sser	'6 persons'

---

[19] I use the more general 'persons' here, although it seems that these terms were usually used for groups of men – compare Stifter: 231.

mórfes(s)er	'7 persons' – this is also an exception and one of my favorite words. Literally, it means 'a great six' and it is a compound of *mór* + *se(i)sser*. You might be surprised to see the letter *f* here. The reason for this *f* has been discussed above, in the section on *r*-stems, regarding the the word *siur*, of which the lenited form is *fiur* (i.e., it goes back to old *sw-*).
ochtar	'8 persons'
nónbur	'9 persons'
de(i)chenbor	'10 persons'

Two - ten things

Groups of things are expressed by adding *–de* to the numeral: *dé(i)de, tré(i)de, cethard(a)e, cóicde, sé(i)de, sechtae, ochtae, noíde, deichde* (all *io,n*; a single thing, for those of you interested, is *úathad*)

And that was it for the numerals. On to the pronouns!

V. PRONOUNS

In this section, the various kinds of personal pronouns in Old Irish are discussed. A personal pronoun is a pronoun referring to a person (I bet you never would have guessed that). The regular personal pronouns in English are I, you, he, she, it, we, you, and they. In an early Irish text, you may find (1) **independent pronouns** (so pronouns that stand alone); (2) **infixed pronouns** (pronouns that are placed in a verbal form); (3) **suffixed pronouns** (pronouns attached to a verb); (4) **possessive pronouns** (these indicate possession – really!); (5) **emphasizing pronouns** (used, as the term already says, for special emphasis), (6) the **combination** of preposition + pronoun; (7) the **anaphoric pronoun** (expressing 'the last-mentioned') and finally (8) the **interrogative pronoun** ('who'etc.). I will discuss them all below.

V.a. Independent (personal) pronouns
(*GOI*: §§405-8, 443, 445-50; Lehmann: 28, 111; McCone: 53-5; Quin: lesson 26; Stifter: 170-1; Strachan: 25; Tigges: 23-4)

Independent pronouns are pronouns that stand by themselves (duh-doy!). Independent pronouns are widely used in many languages these days, including Modern Irish, but they were only used in very specific cases in Old Irish. The basic principle of the independent pronoun in Old Irish is fairly simple:

> There is an independent pronoun for each person (so for 'I', 'you', 'he', 'she', 'it', 'we', 'you' and 'they'). These pronouns have no other forms. When used with verbs, independent pronouns are used **only with the copula**. If you deal with *any* other verb, the person is either already included in the verb, or you use an infixed pronoun (like *dom-beir*).

These are the different forms of the independent pronoun:

Sg. 1. *mé* 'I'
     2. *tú* 'you'
     3.m. *é* 'he' (and NOT *sé*, like in Modern Irish)
     3.f. *sí* 'she' (*í*, like you sometimes get in Modern Irish, is a Middle Irish development)
     3.n. *ed* 'it'

66

Pl. 1. *sní* 'we'
    2. *sí* 'you'
    3. *é* 'they'

If you want to, you can sometimes put extra emphasis on the independent pronoun by adding an extra emphasizing pronoun (for which see section V.e. below):

Sg. 1. *messe*   'me'
    2. *tussu*   'you'
    3.m. *ésom*   'he'
    3.f. *si(s)si*   'she'
    3.n. *ed*   'it'
Pl. 1. *snisni/ sisni/ sinni*   'we'
    2. *sib/ sissi*   'you'
    3. *é*   'they'

Independent pronouns are mostly used in three types of sentences:

(1) In so-called **cleft sentences**, that is to say, in sentences where the independent pronoun is brought forward as the subject or object of the sentence for emphasis (see section VIII.f. below):

    *Is **mé** do-**gní** insin*   'It is *I* who do that'

The independent pronoun is the subject of the cleft sentence (that is to say, if you were to re-write the sentence without 'who', you would get 'I do that', and of that sentence, 'I' is the subject). Note that the verbal form stands in the **third person singular**, NOT in the first person singular. In fact, in this construction, the third person singular is used for **all persons except for the third person plural**!

    *Is **tú** marbas in fer*   'It is *you* whom the man kills'

The independent pronoun is here the **object of the cleft   sentence** (that is, if we were to rewrite the sentence without the relative part, you would get 'the man kills you', and 'you' is the direct object of that sentence).

(2) It is used in combination with ***inso*** and ***insin*** (see below, section VI.b.) to express 'this/that is the x who/that does y'. Note that the **person** and **gender** of the pronoun has to **correspond with the noun** following *inso/insin*:

Is **é** *inso* **in fer** *gaibes claideb*	'*This* is the man who grabs a sword'
Is **ed** *insin* **ainm** *in maicc*	'*That* is the name of the boy'
It **é** *inso* **in maicc** *carmae*	'*These* are the boys whom we love'
Is **sí** *insin* **in túath** *file i n-Érinn*	'*That* is the tribe which is in Ireland'

(3) It can be used without a verb in questions such as *cé* **hé?** 'Who is he?'

V.b. Infixed Pronouns
(*GOI*: §§409-27, 455; Lehmann: 28-9, 34-5; McCone: 55-6; Quin: lessons 11, 23, 33, 36; Stifter: 122-5, 139-40, 186-8, 380; Strachan: 26-8; Tigges: 68-71)

An infixed pronoun is, as the name suggests, a (personal) pronoun that is stuck ('infixed') in a verb. It is used most commonly when the personal pronoun is the **direct object** of a sentence (in English me, you, him, her, it, us, you or them). Some examples: 'he sees **me**'; 'they will hit **you** over the head with a club'. See that in these sentences the direct object is a personal pronoun ('me' and 'you' respectively)?

In Old Irish, there are actually three classes of infixed pronouns, imaginatively titled class A, class B and class C. So when do you use which?

---

class A infixed pronouns are used after preverbs and particles that **originally ended in a vowel**, like *no*, *do*, and *ní*;
class B is used after preverbs and particles that **originally ended in a consonant**, like *as* and *in*;
class C is basically used in **relative clauses**.

Before I will go on to give you the forms of the infixed pronouns of the different classes, I need to talk more in-depth about where they go in the verb – 'stuck inside a verb' is a little bit too vague, isn't it? So where do they go? This will get a bit tricky since I have to start saying things about the verb, which isn't discussed in this book until later on. I will do my best to make it as easy as I can, but you might want to consider reading at least the beginning sections of the chapter on the verb if you have not done so already.

Basically, the infixed pronouns are inserted **directly before the stress of the verb** (this is usually the first syllable of the verbal stem). Old Irish verbs basically have two forms: **independent forms** and **dependent forms** (see the section on the verb for more information). Independent forms are (to put it simply, as there are some exceptions) verbal forms with nothing in front of them; dependent forms are verbal forms preceded by so-called **conjunct particles**, like *ní* 'not', *ma* 'if' and so on.[20]

The **independent** forms are either **absolute** (in simple verbs, that is, verbs that only consist of a verbal root + ending) or **deuterotonic** (in compound verbs, that is, verbs that consist of preverb(s) + verbal root + ending; in these, the stress comes right after the first preverb on the second syllable); the dependent forms are either **conjunct** (in simple verbs) or **prototonic** (in compound verbs; the stress falls on the first syllable).

When you are dealing with the dependent, that is, the conjunct or prototonic form of the verb, you put the infixed pronoun **immediately after the conjunct particle**. Take the verbal forms *ní beir* 'he does not carry' and *ní tabair* 'he does not bring/give'. The conjunct particle *ní* is unstressed. Generally, you only find a maximum of one unstressed particle before the stress. The stress then falls on the next syllable. This means that in these verbal forms, the stress falls on –***beir*** and –***ta***- respectively.

So if you have *ní beir* or *ní tabair*, you insert the infixed pronoun directly before the stress, that is to say, immediately after the conjunct particle, to which it is attached (in both examples, this particle is *ní*). To use a formula, where 'X' indicates the infixed pronoun:

*ní***X**-*beir*	'he doesn't carry X'
*ní***X**-*tabair*	'he doesn't bring/give X'

Now for the independent forms. If you are dealing with the **deuterotonic form** of the verb, you place the infixed pronoun **after the first preverb**, that is, again, immediately before the stress (the first preverb is unstressed). In the verbal form *do-beir* 'he brings/gives', the stress falls on –*beir*. *do-**beir***. Following the same principle as above, we now insert the infixed pronoun (again, I use a formula here where X represents the infixed pronoun):

*do***X**-*beir*	'he brings/gives X'

I hope you are still following me. Now, we have one verbal form left, namely the **absolute form of the verb**. What about that form? Well, there is an issue there. The absolute form of the verb consists of a verbal stem + ending, and nothing else. The stress falls on the first syllable (e.g. ***marb**aid*

---

[20] David Stifter gives a supremely handy overview of all conjunct particles in his book, see p. 135.

'he kills'). This then means that there is nowhere for us to insert the infixed pronoun. Luckily, the Old Irish were crafty. If they needed a pronoun, they either stuck it all the way at the end of the verbal form, so after the –*aid* in *marb**aid*** - this is called a **suffixed pronoun**, and we will get to that in a bit – or they used a **conjunct particle** to which they attached the **infixed pronoun**.

This second option concerns us here. The particle that they used in order to insert the infixed pronoun is the particle *no*. This particle is meaningless (that is to say, you do not translate it), and you will find it time and again, not just to accommodate infixed pronouns. My former lecturer at Utrecht University, Leni van Strien, used to call *no* a coat-rack particle – a particle that is there purely for you to hang things on if there are no other conjunct particles available. Since *no* is a conjunct particle, the absolute form **changes into a conjunct form**.

To give an example: we have just seen the absolute verbal form *marbaid* 'he kills'. If you want to say something like 'he kills **X**' (X representing a personal pronoun here, i.e. me, you, him, her, it, us you or them), what do you do? Well, we do not have a preverb or conjunct particle that we can tack the infixed pronoun onto, so we will have to use the particle *no*. I have just said that *no* is a conjunct particle, and it is followed by the conjunct form here. So then all you need to know that the conjunct form we need is *marba*. Now you just have to insert the infixed pronoun (X) after *no* and before *marba*:

> *no***X**-*marba*   'he kills **X**'

See how easy that was? High time to take a peek at the three classes of infixed pronouns.

V.b.1. Infixed pronouns class A
(*GOI*: 411, 415-6; Lehmann: 28-9, 34; McCone: 55-6; Quin: lesson 11; Stifter: 122-5, 380; Strachan: 26-7; Tigges: 69-70)

As already stated, you find the infixed pronoun class A after preverbs and particles that originally ended in a vowel. Here are the forms of the infixed pronoun of class A and some examples of what they look like:

Person		Form	Mutation	Meaning	Example	Translation
Sg.	1.	*-m*	lenites	'me'	*do**m**-beir*	he brings **me**
	2.	*-t*	lenites	'you'	*no**t**-charam*	we love **you**
Sg.	3. m.	*-a*	nasalizes	'him'	*ní-**m**biur*	I do not carry **him**
	3.f.	*-s*	(nasalizes)	'her'	*no**s**-léicet*	they allow **her**
	3.n.	*-a*	lenites	'it'	*da-gní*	he does **it**
Pl.	1.	*-n*	nothing	'us'	*no**n**-marbai*	you kill **us**
	2.	*-b*	nothing	'you'	*no**b**-moraim*	I praise **you**
	3.	*-s*	(nasalizes)	'them'	*ní**s**-aicci*	she does not see **them**

The infixed pronouns in the third person singular feminine and in the third person plural can nasalize, but they don't have to and don't always do it.

Now, the forms of the infixed pronoun in the third person singular masculine and neuter is *–a* (a nasalizing *a* for the masculine infixed pronoun and a leniting *a* for the neuter infixed pronoun, if you want to be exact).

If the particle that the infixed pronoun 3 sg. m/n is attached to ends in the letter *–o*, like *do, no* and *fo*, the *–a* wins out and the *–o* disappears. An example: *do-gní*, 'he makes', *da-gní*, 'he makes it'.

However, if infixed pronouns are added to the conjunct particle *ní*, the *–í* is stronger and wins out, and the *–a* **disappears completely**. An example: *ní beir*, 'he does not carry' **or** 'he does not carry it'; *ní-mbeir*, 'he does not carry him'. In this final case, you can see that *ní* consists of the negative particle *ní* + the infixed pronoun class A 3 sg. m. *a*, because the *a* nasalizes the following verbal form *m**beir*.

This is a bit tricky, because this means that you will always have to look and see if the verbal form that comes after *ní* has been lenited or nasalized. And of course, sometimes, you will not see it at all, since not all the consonants show lenition or nasalization, as you well know. Do not worry though. Usually, it is clear from the context whether there is an infixed pronoun there or not. Just remember for now that even though you do not always see it, there *can* be an infixed pronoun of the third person singular masculine or neuter after *ní*.

It is also really, really important to remember that the **infixed pronoun** generally expresses the **direct object** (accusative) and NOT the subject.

So my advice to avoid confusion: if you have to translate a verb form with an infixed pronoun in it, first translate the verbal form, and **only then** look at the infixed pronoun. For example: if you have the form *nín-chara*, first translate *ní chara*, 'he does not love', and then look at the infixed pronoun, -*n* 'us'. The outcome of *nín-chara* is therefore 'he does not love us'.

Let us try another one; *da-mbiur*. First look at the verbal form, which is *do-biur*, 'I bring'. The infixed pronoun is –*a* and it nasalizes the following stressed word. From the overview above, you can see that that is an infixed pronoun in the third person singular masculine 'him'. So the outcome of *da-mbiur* is 'I bring him'.

One final example: *nos-léicem*. The verbal form is –*léicem* (with *no* being that meaningless particle), 'we allow'. The infixed pronoun is –*s*, so that can be either third person singular feminine 'her' or third person plural 'them' – in a text you have to look at the context to decide which one fits. So this one can mean either 'we allow her' or 'we allow them'. And that is pretty much all there is to it!

There is one other special use of the infixed pronoun that I need to point out, and here is as good a place as anywhere. As you may know already, there is no specific verb for 'to have' in Old Irish. So how do they express that? They do this by using a special dependent form of the substantive verb (one of the verbs expressing 'to be' – see section IX): -*tá* (in the meaning 'there is').

In Old Irish, infixed pronouns can be used with –*tá* to indicate possession, to whom something belongs, e.g. 'there is **to me**' = 'I have', 'there is **to you**' = 'you have'. This infixed pronoun does not function as a direct object, but as an **indirect object** (a dative, if you will). Let's look at the paradigm:

*no**m**-thá*	'I have' (literally 'there is to me')
*no**t**-tá*	'You have' (lit. 'there is to you')
na-tá	'He has' (lit. 'there is to him')
nos-tá	'She has' (lit. 'there is to her')
na-thá	'It has' (lit. 'there is to it')
*no**n**-tá*	'We have' (lit. 'there is to us')
*no**b**-tá*	'You (pl.) have' (lit. 'there is to you')
nos-tá	'They have' (lit. 'there is to them')

Note: do not confuse this with the infixed pronouns with –***fil***, the more regular dependent form of the substantive verb in the present indicative! That is used to express 'X is/am/are not', e.g. *nim-fil* 'I am not', *nín-fil* 'we are not' etc. For forms with –*fil*, see chapter IX .

V.b.2. Infixed pronouns class B

(*GOI*: §§412, 414-5, 417; Lehmann: 28-9; McCone: 55-6; Quin: lesson 23; Stifter: 139-40, 380; Strachan: 26-7; Tigges: 69-70)

Alright. Now, I have just discussed infixed pronouns class A, which are used after particles and preverbs that originally ended in a vowel. Logically, infixed pronouns class B are used after particles and preverbs that originally ended in a **consonant**. Makes sense, doesn't it? Some examples of preverbs that are followed by infixed pronouns class B: *etar-*, *for-*, *fri-* or *frith-*, *con-* or *com-*, *ad-*, *aith-*, *ess-*, and *in(d)-*.

A few notes: when *fri-* or *frith-* is used with an infixed pronoun, the preverb changes to *frit-* (so *fritom-* etc.). When *con-* or *com-* is combined with the infixed pronoun, it changes to *cot-*. The last four preverbs I just mentioned, *ad-*, *aith-*, *ess-* (often *as-*), and *in(d)-* all change to ***at-*** when used with a pronoun. This can be very tricky when you are looking up verbal forms in *DIL*, so remember this!

Now, let's take a look at the forms of the infixed pronoun class B used with the verb *ad-cí* 'sees' (and note that *ad-* has changed to *at-*):

Person		Form	Mutation	Example	Translation
Sg.	1.	*-dom/ -tom* *-dam/ -tam*	lenites	*a**tom**-chí*	he sees **me**
	2.	*-tot/ -tut*	lenites	*a**tot**-chíat*	they see **you**
	3. m.	*-t*	nasalizes	*at-**cítis***	they saw **him**
	3. f.	*-da/ -ta*	h-mutation	*a**ta**-cíu*	I see **her**
	3. n.	*-t*	lenites	*at-**chítis***	they saw **it**
Pl.	1.	*-don/ -ton/ -dan*	--------	*co**ton**-dieig*	he asks **us**
	2.	*-dob/ -dub/ -tob*	--------	*a**tob**-cíd*	she saw **you**
	3.	*-da/ -ta*	h-mutation	*a**ta**-cíu*	I see **them**

Note that as in infixed pronouns class A, the feminine 3 singular and the 3 plural forms look alike, and that the 3 sg. masculine and neuter only differ in the mutation they cause – so don't forget to look at the following word. If the following word begins with a letter that does not show lenition or nasalization, you will have to figure out which of the two it is by looking at the context.

V.b.3. Infixed pronouns class C
(*GOI*: §§413, 414-5,418; Lehmann: 28-9; McCone: 55-6; Quin: lesson 33; Stifter: 186-8, 380; Strachan: 26-7; Tigges: 69-70)

This brings us to the final class of infixed pronouns: class C. First, I will give you the different forms. Note that they look very similar to the ones used for the infixed pronouns class B:

Person		Form	Mutation	Example	Translation
Sg.	1.	*dom-/ dam-*	lenites	*dian**dom** accai*	If you see **me**
	2.	*dot-/ dat-/ dit-*	lenites	*con**dot** biur*	So that I bring **you**
	3.m.	*id-/ did-/ d-*	nasal.	*con**id** n-accae*	So that she saw **him**
	3.f.	*da*	h-mut.	*in tan ro-n-**da**-icc*	When he reaches **her**
	3.n.	*id-/ did-/ d-*	lenites	*con**id** accae*	So that she saw **it**
Pl.	1.	*don-/ dun-/ dan*	-----	*con**don** bir*	So that you bring **us**
	2.	*dob-/ dub-/ dab*	-----	*in tan do-n-**dob**-bered*	When he gave **you**
	3.	*da*	h-mut.	*con**da** accae*	So that he saw **them**

The infixed pronoun class C is most commonly used in relative clauses. To be more specific, it is used in the following four cases:

1. In relative clauses, where it **replaces infixed pronouns class A** (so when you have a relative clause in which the particle or preverb originally ended in a vowel). Sometimes, the infixed pronoun class A is *not* replaced with a class C infixed pronoun in the first and second persons singular and plural – but never mind that for now.

Infixed pronouns class C are also often used in relative clauses, where they replace the **third person singular and the third person plural** of a **class B** infixed pronoun. The other persons of the class B pronoun are generally not replaced in a relative sentence. This all sounds overly complicated, so let me give you a few examples to illustrate what I just said:

Non-relative	Relative
*Do**m**-beir cosin n-insi*	*In fer do**dam**-beir cosin n-insi*
'He carries **me** to the island'	'The man who carries **me** to the island'
(infixed pronoun class A)	(infixed pronoun class C)
*A**t**-beir*	*Intí as-**id**-beir*
'He says **it**'	'He who says **it**'
(infixed pronoun class B)	(infixed pronoun class C)

74

2. The infixed pronoun class C is used after (conjunctions that are followed by) relative nasalization (see section VIII.c), for example *in tan ro-n-**dom**-icc* 'when he reaches **me**', *con**id** accae* 'so that he saw it'.

3. It is used after the **interrogative particle** *in*: *in**dam** beir cosin n-insi?* 'Does he carry me to the island?'

4. It is used after a **preposition combined with the relative particle** *a* (and this relative particle causes nasalization), like *dia,* 'from whom, from which' *lassa,* 'by whom, by which'.

V.b.4. The infixed pronoun combined with the relative and imperative negations *nád* and *ná*

(*GOI*: §419; Lehmann: - ; McCone: 55-6; Quin: lesson 36; Stifter: 187-8; Strachan: 27; Tigges: 71)

The relative and imperative negations *nád* (with relative clauses – see chapter VIII) and *ná* (before the imperative – for the imperative see chapter VII.b.3. below) are often combined with the infixed pronoun. This is what the forms look like (basically, they look like *ná* + *ch* + infixed pronouns class A, with the exception of the 3 sg. f. and the 3 pl., that look like infixed pronouns class B, and 3 sg. m. and one of the forms for 3 sg. n, where there is no ending):

Negative + pronoun		Mutation	Example	Translation
Sg.	1. *náchim, nácham*	lenites	*náchim marbad*	Let him not kill **me**!
	2. *náchit, náchat*	lenites	*intí náchat marb*	He who does not kill **you**
	3.m. *nách*	nasal.	*nách marbam*	Let us not kill **him**!
	3.f. *nácha*	h-mut.	*intí nácha marbad*	He who did not kill **her**
	3.n. *nách, náchid*	lenites	*nách epir!*	Do not say **it**!
Pl.	1. *náchin, náchan*	none	*náchan marb!*	Do not kill **us**!
	2. *náchib, náchab*	none	*intí náchib marb*	He who does not kill **you**
	3. *nácha*	h-mut.	*nácha marb!*	Do not kill **them**!

V.c. Suffixed Pronouns

(*GOI*: §§428-31; Lehmann: 35; McCone: 55-6; Quin: lesson 34; Stifter: 295-6; Strachan: 25; Tigges: 44, 58-9)

As if there aren't enough pronouns flying around in your head already, there is another type of pronoun we need to discuss (I mentioned it briefly earlier): the **suffixed pronoun**. Suffixed pronouns are usually found in earlier texts and disappear in the Middle Irish period. In fact, even in Old Irish they only occur under very specific circumstances. Before I get around to those, here is the important information to remember:

> Suffixed pronouns are pronouns that are **attached** (suffixed) to the **absolute form** of the verb. They express the direct object.

This means they **only** occur with **simple verbs**, and only in the **absolute**. They are most commonly used instead of an infixed pronoun to express the direct object of a verb **after the 3 sg. absolute**. The only other forms of the verb to which a suffixed pronoun is attached are the 3 pl. forms ending in –*it*, the 1 pl. forms ending in –*mi*, and the 1 sg. future ending in –*a*. The suffixed pronoun then used is **only** that of 3 sg. masculine or neuter, and it takes the form –*it* instead of the usual –*i*. In **all other cases**, you will find the infixed pronoun. In verbal forms with a suffixed pronoun attached, look for syncope, as that will happen very often.

These are the forms you might find:

		Attached to 3 sg. absolute:	Example	Translation
Sg.	1.	-*um*	*beirthi***um**	(s)he/it carries **me**
	2.	-*ut*	*beirthi***ut**	(s)he/it carries **you** (sg.)
	3.m.	-*i*	*beirthi*	(s)he/it carries **him**
	3.f.	-*us*	*beirthi***us**	(s)he/it carries **her**
	3.n.	-*i*	*beirthi*	(s)he/it carries **it**
Pl.	1.	-*unn*	*beirthi***unn**	(s)he/it carries **us**
	2.	-*uib*	*beirth***uib**	(s)he/it carries **you** (pl.)
	3.	-*us*	*beirthi***us**	(s)he/it carries **them**

		Attached to 3 pl. in –*it*/ 1 pl. in –*mi*; 1 sg. fut in –*a*:	Example	Translation
Sg.	1.	-	-	
	2.	-	-	

Sg. 3.m.	*-it*	*berta**it***	they carry **him**
		*marbma**it***	we kill **him**
3.f.	-		
3.n.	*-it*	*rega**it***	I will go **it***
Pl. 1.	-		
2.	-		
3.	-		

* In English, you can just translate this with 'I will go'.

Now, let's see how this suffixing process works. Let's look at the examples in the overview above found after absolute verbal forms 3 sg. All of the examples have been made with the verbal form *beirid*, 'he carries'. If you want to say 'he carries it', you could of course use an infixed pronoun, giving you *na-beir*; but we are not going to, since this is the section on suffixed pronouns. First, you take the form *beirid*, then you add the ending for the third person singular neuter, which as you can see above, is *–i*: **beirid-i*. However, this would give us three syllables, which can only mean one thing: SYNCOPE! As you hopefully know, we lose the *i* of the second syllable, meaning that the group that remains behind would become palatal. This gives us **beirdi*.

However, the form you will find in a text is actually *beirthi*. That is a bit unexpected, but it makes sense if I tell you that early on in Old Irish, the verb ending for the third person singular absolute was actually *–(a)ith*, and not *–(a)id* (in fact, in early texts like the *Cambrai Homily* you can still find forms like *beirith* 'he carries'), and this is a case where you still see that old ending.

Let's try another one. Let's translate 'he releases them'. You take the 3 sg. absolute present indicative of *léicid*, which is of course *léicid*, and add the suffixed pronoun 3 pl., which is *–us*. Again, remember syncope and that older ending, and we get **léicid-us*, **léicdius*, resulting in the form **léicthius**.

One more important point: the suffixed pronoun can also be used with the **substantive verb**. This suggests that originally, the substantive verb was a simple verb, because compound verbs, as I said, cannot take suffixed pronouns. Food for thought. Or not, if that makes it more confusing. In that case, ignore what I just said for now and move on.

As is the case with the infixed pronouns combined with the substantive verb, if you use a suffixed pronoun with the substantive verb, it functions as a dative, or an indirect object, meaning 'there is to me' = 'I have':

		+ Infixed Pronoun	+ Suffixed Pronoun	Translation
Sg.	1.	*nom-thá*	*táth**um***	I have
	2.	**not-tá*	*táth**ut***	you have
	3.m.	**na-tá*	*táthai*	he has
	3.f.	*nos-tá*	*táth**us***	she has
	3.n.	**na-tá*	*táthai*	it has
Pl.	1.	*non-tá*	*táithi**unn***	we have
	2.	*nob-tá*	*táth**uib***	you (pl.) have
	3.	*nos-tá*	*táth**us***	they have

V.d. Possessive pronouns

(*GOI*: §§438-44; Lehmann: 19, 35; McCone: 54; Quin: lesson 17; Stifter: 69-70; Strachan: -; Tigges: 23-5)

Possessive pronouns, as the name already implies, indicate possession. The possessive pronouns in English are *my, your, him, her, its, our, your, their* (e.g. my book, your dog, his shoe, her house, its color, our grades, your shirts and their holidays). This is what they look like:

		Form	Mutation	Example	Translation
Sg.	1.	*mo*	lenites	*mo chenn*	my head
	2.	*do*	lenites	*do thech*	your house
	3.m.	*a*	lenites	*a charae*	his friend
	f.	*a*	h-mutation	*a ech*	her horse
	n.	*a*	lenites	*a chride*	its heart
Pl.	1.	*ar*	nasalizes	*ar n-inis*	our island
	2.	*far/for*	nasalizes	*far nguidi*	your prayers
	3.	*a*	nasalizes	*a n-eich*	their horses

That is not too bad now, is it? Especially for those of you who know Modern Irish, since they are basically the same. The possessive pronouns of the first and second person singular, *mo* and *do*, can change into *m'* and *t'* if they come before a vowel, as in *t'ainm*, 'your name'. And that is basically it.

V.e. Emphasizing pronouns

(*GOI*: §§403-4; Lehmann: 28, 37; McCone: 53; Quin: lesson 23; Stifter: 127-8; Strachan: 24-5; Tigges: 38)

Now, on to another kind of pronoun: *emphasizing pronouns*, also known as emphasizing particles. As the name suggests, you use emphasizing pronouns to put emphasis on something. They are fairly easy – especially since emphasizing pronouns are still used in Modern Irish. Emphasizing pronouns can basically be used in five ways:

1. to put emphasis on a **possessive pronoun**:
   *mo chenn-***sa** '*my* head' (compare *mo chota-sa* in Modern Irish);
2. to emphasize an **infixed pronoun**:
   *dom-beir-***sa**, 'he carries *me*' (compare *liom-sa* in Modern Irish);
3. to emphasize the **subject which is included in the verb   ending**:
   *dom-beir-***sium**, '*he* carries me';
4. to emphasize the **subject of the copula** (the copula, you may remember, is one of the two verbs expressing 'to be' in Old Irish – see chapter IX below). The emphasizing pronoun is attached to **the predicate** of the sentence (the predicate is that part of a copula sentence that gives you additional information about   the subject – see chapter IX below). The reason for this is that the copula itself is unstressed, and so   is the emphasizing pronoun. Since you can't really have two subsequent unstressed words, you need to attach the emphasizing pronoun to another word that *is* stressed, like the predicate. An example: *am rígain-***se** '*I* am queen';
5. Lastly, the emphasizing pronoun can be attached to the independent (that is, free standing) personal pronouns, for   extra emphasis (see the section on the independent personal pronoun above).

The forms of the emphasizing pronoun that you may encounter in your texts are:

Sg.			Pl.		
1.	*-sa, -se*		1.	*-ni*	
2.	*-so, -su, -siu*		2.	*-si*	
3.m.	*-som, -sem, -sium*		3.	*-som, -sium, -sem*	
3.f.	*-si*				
3.n.	*-som, -sem*				

Note that the forms for the 3 sg. feminine and the 2 pl. look the same. If you were to see a form like *dos-beirid-si*, you will have to look at the context to determine whether this means 'you carry *her*' or '*you* carry her' (and it is possible that you will still be unable to figure it out then – in a way this is good, because either way, you are correct). The same goes for the 3 sg. masculine and neuter and the 3 plural.

The forms in which the *s*- is neutral (*-sa, -so, -som* etc.) generally follow a word ending in a neutral vowel or consonant; if the preceding word ended in a palatal (or slender) vowel or consonant, the other forms of the emphasizing pronoun (where the *s*- is palatal as in *–se, -siu, -si* etc.) are generally used.

79

V.f. The anaphoric pronoun *suide, side*
(*GOI*: §§477, 479; Lehmann: -; McCone: 53; Quin: -; Stifter: 190; Strachan: 203; Tigges: -)

In early Irish texts, you will often encounter the stressed word *suide* (the neuter form nom./acc. is *sodain*), or the unstressed forms *side* (3 sg. m.), *ade* (3 sg. f.), (*s*)*ón* (3 sg. n.) and the 3 plural forms *side, sidi, adi, ade*. These unstressed forms are attached to a pronoun or the subject of a copula clause; the stressed forms are often used after prepositions. This pronoun, called 'anaphoric' refers back to a person or thing that has been mentioned (immediately) before, and its basic translation is 'the latter, the aforementioned', e.g. *Is rí Conn. Is é-side cartae inna mná.* 'Conn is a king; it is the aforementioned whom the women love'.

V.g. The combination of preposition + personal pronoun
(*GOI*: §§432-7; Lehmann: 19, 35, 61-3, 129; McCone: 58-61; Quin: lesson 17; Stifter: 87-90; Strachan: 29-33; Tigges: 36-8)

We have already seen that in Old Irish, if you wish to express a direct object, you would normally use an infixed/suffixed pronoun; but if you wish to express things other than the direct object ('to me', 'with me', that kind of thing), you would pretty much always use a preposition (the indirect object thing that I discussed with the substantive verb is really an exception). Now rather than using a preposition followed by a pronoun like *do mé*, Irish combines the preposition and the pronoun, giving you *dom*, 'to me'. The pattern is basically this:

Letter(s) added to preposition:
Sg. 1.   - *m*
2.   - *t*
3.   there is no fixed rule for the third person singular; there are a lot of different possibilities, so it is best to just learn this while translating.
Pl. 1.   - *n*(*n*)
2.   - palatal *b*
3.   - palatal *b* if the preposition is followed by a dative;
     - *u* if the preposition is followed by the accusative.

The combinations will look something like this: *dom* 'to me', *it* 'to you', *duit* 'to you', *liom* 'with me', *friu* 'against them', *dó* 'for him', *fort* 'on you', *doib* 'to them'. Sometimes a vowel is added, as in *cucunn* 'to us'. For the people who have studied Modern Irish, this section should be especially easy, since this still exists in Modern Irish (think of sentences like *cad is ainm* **duit?** 'what is your name' and *tá ocras* **orm** 'I am hungry').

I want to mention one thing for those of you who are using Strachan's *Paradigms*. In the section of prepositions which can be followed by *either a dative or an accusative* (*Paradigms* pages 32 and 33), you find the letters D. and A. after the third person singular and the third person plural. D. means dative and is followed by the form you get when the preposition is followed by a dative (like in the sentence 'The island? We are standing on it.' – the dative expresses a sense of rest); A. means accusative and is followed by the form you get when the preposition is followed by the accusative, like: 'The horse? He is loading his bags onto it' (the accusative expresses a sense of motion).

V.h. Other expressions

V.h.1. The expression 'self'

(*GOI*: §§485; Lehmann: -; McCone: 54; Quin: -; Stifter: -, but cp. 93; Strachan: 33; Tigges: 38)

There are a few different words in Old Irish to express '-self' ('myself', 'the man himself' etc. – this is sometimes referred to as a 'reflexive pronoun'), and there are different forms for different persons, as you can see in the overview below. These words can be used:

  (1) after a possessive or personal pronoun (*mo brat féin* 'my own cloak', *mé féin* 'I myself');
  (2) after an article + noun (*in fer fesin* 'the man himself'),
  (3) after a proper name (*Medb feisne* 'Medb herself'), or
  (4) as the subject of a clause (*marbaid fesin* 'he himself kills').

Thurneysen provides the following forms (*GOI* §485):

		Form	Example
Sg.	1.	*féin/céin/fadéin/cadéin*	*mé féin* '(I) myself'
	2.	*féin/céin/fadéin/cadéin*	*tú féin* '(you) yourself'
	3. m/n	*féin/fe(i)(s)sin/fade(is)sin/ fadéne/cesin/cadesin*	*in fer fesin* 'the man himself'
	3. f.	*fe(i)sine/feisne/f(e)is(s)in*	*Medb feissin* 'Medb herself'
Pl.	1.	*fesine/fanisin/canisin*	*sní fanisin* '(us) ourselves'
	2.	*feis(s)ne/fesin/fadeisne/ fadisin/*cadeisne/*cadisin*	*sibh fadeisne* '(you pl.) yourselves'
	3.	*fe(i)s(s)(i)ne/fe(is)sin/fade(i)s(i)ne/ fadesin/fedesin/ceisne/cades(si)ne/ cadesin*	*a n-eich fadesin* 'their own horses'

V.h.2. The expression '(an)other'

(*GOI*: §§486-8; Lehmann: - ; McCone: - ; Quin: -; Stifter: 81, 143; Strachan: - ; Tigges: -)

The expression '(an)other' ('other horses', 'another one' etc.) has both an adjectival and a substantival form. If it is used as an **adjective**, the form is *aile* (m/f) and *aill* (n.), it is found (as you would expect) after a noun, and it is declined like an *io,iā*-stem adjective) e.g. *don macc ailiu* 'for the other son'.

As with other adjectives, it can be used **substantivally with the article** (e.g. *int aile, a n-aill* 'the other', in which the first example, *int aile* refers to a masculine person/object, and *a n-aill* refers to a neuter object (you can see this in the form of the article as well as the form of *aill/ aile*).

The more regular **substantival form**, the one used **without the article**, is *alaile* or *araile* (masculine/feminine) and *alaill/ araill* (neuter; this will lenite a following word), with stress on the second syllable (so *al-AILL*).

Note: occasionally, you will also find *alaile/ araile/ alaill/ araill* used in an adjectival sense, e.g. *alaile macc* 'another son'

V.h.3. The expression 'each, every, everyone, everything'

(*GOI*: §§490; Lehmann: -; McCone: - ; Quin: -; Stifter: 81; Strachan: - ; Tigges: -)

The **adjectival form** (so 'every/each' in 'every man', 'each syllable' etc.) is *cach* or *cech* for all genders and in all cases, except genitive singular feminine *cacha/ cecha* (rarely, you will find a genitive neuter *caich*). It stands **before** the noun. The initial *c* is never lenited, not even after prepositions that would normally lenite, so *do cach macc* 'for every son' etc.

Plural forms expressing 'all' (so 'all men, all women' etc.) are rare, and usually end in *a*, so *cacha túatha* 'all tribes', although sometimes, the *a* is omitted and you will just find *cach/ cech*.

The **substantival form** in masculine/feminine ('everyone') is *cách*, with a length-mark. This is the form found in the nominative, accusative and dative. The form of the genitive ends in a palatal consonant group, *cáich*. If you want to say 'everything', you use the adjectival form *cach* followed by the substantive *ní* 'something', so *cach ní* 'everything' (for the form *ní* 'something', see V.h.4. below).

V.h.4. The expression 'any, some, anyone, anything, someone, something' (a.k.a. indefinite pronouns)
(*GOI*: §§489; Lehmann: - ; McCone: - ; Quin: -; Stifter: 189; Strachan: - ; Tigges: -)

The **adjectival** form 'any, some' ('any man, some bread' etc.), stands before the noun and is *nach* if followed by a masculine or feminine word, and *na* if followed by a neuter word. *Nach* is the form usually found in the singular in all cases except for the nominative and accusative neuter form *na*, and the genitive feminine *nacha*. Like *cach*, the plural forms found end almost always in *a*, so the form you can expect to find is *nacha*.

If used **substantivally**, the forms are *nech* ('someone, anyone', the same form for both masculine and feminine) and *ní* 'something, anything' (neuter). The attested form in the genitive singular is *neich*, in dat. sg. *neuch/neoch*.

V.i. Interrogative pronouns
(*GOI*: §§456-62; Lehmann: ; McCone: - ; Quin: - ; Stifter: 190; Strachan: -; Tigges: 109)[21]

If you want to ask a question beginning with 'who?' or 'what?' you have to use an interrogative pronoun. This comes in both an unstressed and a stressed form. These forms can stand:

(1) on their own, before the verb
(2) before a noun/personal pronoun

If they stand before a **verbal form**:
The unstressed form is *ce/ci/cia* (the same for all genders!), and it is a conjunct particle (i.e., it is followed by the conjunct/prototonic form of the verb). It is important to note that the unstressed interrogative particle can stand for either **the subject or the object** – so pay close attention to the verbal ending! Some examples: *cia beir?* 'who carries?', *cia berat?* 'what are they carrying?' The stressed forms are *cía* 'who is it'? (masculine and feminine) and neuter *cid* 'what is it'? The plural is *citne* 'who/what are they'?, and these forms are followed by a relative clause (see chapter VIII for these).

---

[21] This section is based on Stifter's discussion. See also interrogative particles below, section VII.g.2.

If they stand before a **noun**:

The unstressed form is the same (so *ce*/*ci*/*cia*). The unstressed forms are often used in combination with nouns to express ideas like 'when' ('what time'), 'how' ('what manner') etc. In the case of the stressed forms, the form used before a masculine word is *cía*, before a feminine word is *cisí* (leniting) and the form before a neuter word is *cid* (leniting), e.g. *cía fer?* 'Who is the man?', *cisí ben?* 'who is the woman?', *cid chenél* 'what is the kindred?'.

In addition to this, there are a number of other interrogative pronouns that you may encounter in texts, such as *cote*/*cate*, pl. *coteat, cateat*, 'what is?', 'what are?'; *coich* 'whose is?', *can* 'whence, from where?' (e.g. in the title *Can a mbunadas na nGoídel*, 'Whence the origin of the Goídil?', a ninth-century poem by Máelmura Othna) and finally *cis lir* 'how many [are there]?' - this formula occurs often in law texts (e.g. *cis lir fodlai aíre* 'How many divisions of satire are there?' - the first line of an early Irish tract on satire – for which see Roisin McLaughlin's book *Early Irish satire*, p. 52ff.).

VI. THE DEICTIC PARTICLE *Í* AND DEMONSTRATIVES

VI.a. The deictic particle *í*
(*GOI*: §§474, 476; Lehmann: -; McCone: 54; Quin: lesson 25; Stifter: 188; Strachan: -; Tigges: -)

The word 'deictic' comes from a Greek verb meaning 'to show', and is used to refer to specific things or persons that you have in mind. Think of it as if you were pointing out someone in a crowd of people, or a specific cupcake in a display case. Although it may look complicated when you first see it, the principle behind the formation of the deictic particle *í* is extremely easy. This is what you should remember:

> The deictic particle *í* is always **unstressed**, is **indeclinable** and is usually **attached to the article**.

It is mainly used in three ways in Old Irish:
1. to refer to a **famous thing or person**(s), or a person mentioned earlier on in a text, expressing things like 'that   famous Cú Chulainn', or 'the aforementioned Queen Medb'.
2. in combination with **demonstratives**, or standing on its own, expressing things like 'these persons', 'those things', 'that person' or for heavy stress – see also the section on demonstratives below;
3. as the **antecedent** of a relative clause (the antecedent is the element in the main clause to which the relative clause refers back (in 'the man who can fly', 'the man' is the antecedent – see also below, section VIII), e.g. 'he who goes to school everyday' (the antecedent there is 'he'; you can almost compare this use to the expressions 'your man' and 'your one' in Hiberno-English, or 'that guy' in American English).

This last usage, of the deictic particle functioning as an antecedent (expressing things like 'he who…'), is the most common of the three.

Now that we know that the deictic particle is attached to the article, things become a lot easier: just attach *–í* to the appropriate form of the article. The same rules apply that we have seen with nouns, e.g. the masculine article in the nominative singular is *in* but *int* if it is followed by a vowel. Because *–í* is a vowel, you would use the form *int*. Also, in instances where the article will nasalize the following word (for example in the nominative singular neuter), you will find an *n-* before the *i*. Since you already know what forms of the article are used in what cases, this should be a piece of cake (otherwise, you should really start memorizing the forms of the article).

Masculine

Singular			**Plural**		
Article	**Article + -*i***		**Article**	**Article + -*i***	
Nom. *in/int*	*int-i* 'he'		*in/ind/int*	*ind-i*	'they'
Acc. *in*	*in n-i* 'him'		*inna*	*inna-i*	'them'
Gen. *in(d/t)*	*ind-i* 'of him'		*inna*	*inna n-i*	'of them'
Dat. *don(d/t)*	*dond-i* 'to him'		*cosnaib*	*cosnaib-i*	'with them'

See, isn't that simple? Now, let us look at the feminine and neuter forms of the article:

Feminine

Note: the plural 'they' in this instance refers to a group of women.

	Singular			**Plural**		
	Article	**Article + -*i***		**Article**	**Article + -*i***	
Nom.	*in(d/t)*	*ind-i* 'she'		*inna*	*inna-i*	'they'
Acc.	*in*	*in n-i* 'her'		*inna*	*inna-i*	'them'
Gen.	*inna*	*inna-i* 'of her'		*inna*	*inna n-i*	'of them'
Dat.	*don(d/t)*	*dond-i* 'to her'		*donaib*	*donaib-i*	'to them'

Neuter

	Singular			**Plural**		
	Article	**Article + -*i***		**Article**	**Article + -*i***	
Nom.	*a*	*a n-i* 'it, the thing'		*inna*	*inna-i*	'the things'
Acc.	*a*	*a n-i* 'it, the thing'		*inna*	*inna-i*	'the things'
Gen.	*in(d/t)*	*ind-i* 'of it'		*inna*	*inna n-i*	'of the things'
Dat.	*don(d/t)*	*dond-i* 'for it'		*donaib*	*donaib-i*	'for the things'

See – nothing irregular about any of it. All you need to do is add one letter to something you have learned ages ago. Let me use some of the forms in some sentences, to make the whole thing crystal-clear for you:

*Téit **int-í** Cú Chulainn co Temair*	- the deictic particle refers
'That famous Cú Chulainn goes to Tara'	to a famous person

Do-beir **inna-í-sin** *cosin n-insi*	- the deictic particle is used in
'She carries those things to the island'	combination with a demonstrative

Ad-cíu ech **ind-í** *beires claideb cosin cath*	- the deictic particle is the
'I see the horse of he (the person)	antecedent of the relative
who carries a sword to the battle'	clause;

Crenmai **inna-í** *carmae*	- the deictic particle is used to
'We buy the things we love'	express the antecedent

A small note: in actual manuscripts, there is no dash (hyphen) between the article part and the deictic particle. In fact, there are no dashes in manuscripts at all, except sometimes at the end of a line to indicate that a word continues on the next line. Editors of texts may choose to use a dash or not, so the way I am writing all of this down here is not necessarily the exact form you will find in a text – be aware of that when you are translating! This does not only apply to the deictic particle, but in all instances where you might find a dash here, like the infixed pronoun or the emphasizing pronoun.

VI.b. Demonstratives
(*GOI*: §§475, 477-82; Lehmann: 37; McCone: 60-1; Quin: lesson 25; Stifter: 102, 129; Strachan: - ; Tigges: 110)

A demonstrative is a particle that is attached to a word to express 'this' or 'that'. The particle used to express 'this' is *so, sa* (after words ending in a neutral letter) or *se, seo, siu* (after words ending in a palatal letter). This particle is **uninflected** and can be used in a number of ways:

1. It can be added to a noun, e.g. *in fer so*, 'this man', *in túath so*, 'this tribe'.
2. It can also be added to the combination of article and deictic particle that we have seen above, like *inna-í-siu*, 'these things', 'these persons'
3. For really heavy stress, you can use the deictic particle *í* with the demonstrative after a noun, e.g. *in ben ísiu*, '*this* woman'
4. It can be used independently with *in* to express 'this': *inso*, 'this'
5. It can be used with prepositions. If the preposition preceding it is followed by a dative, the demonstrative used is *-síu*, e.g. *resíu* 'before this'; if it is followed by an accusative, however, the demonstrative used is *-so,-sa, -se*, e.g. *lasse* 'with this'

The particle used to express 'that' is *sin*. It is used in the same ways as *-so/-se/-siu*. I shall give you some examples:

1. Added to a noun: *in fer sin*, 'that man' *int ech sin*, 'that horse', *in guide sin*, 'that prayer'
2. Used after article + *-í*: *inna-í-sin*, 'those things/people', *dond-í-sin* 'to that person/thing'
3. Used in combination with *–í* after a noun for heavy stress: *in fer ísin*, '*that* man'
4. Used independently with *in*: *insin*, 'that'
5. Used with prepositions: *íar sin*, 'after that' *la sin* 'with that'

Some sentences:

Beir in claideb so cosin fer sin   - demonstrative used after noun
'Carry this sword to that man'

Ad-cítis inna-í-sin   - demonstrative used with article + *-í*
'They saw those things'/
'Those things were seen'

In n-aicci a tech ísin?   - demonstrative used with *í* for heavy
'Do you see that house?'   stress

Run inso. At-beir frisa notairiu   - demonstrative used with '*in*'
'This is a secret (lit. 'a secret this').
He tells it to his scribes.'

Téit cosa tech íar sin   - demonstrative used after preposition
'He goes to the house after that'

Note: if you want to express a sense of distance in time or in place, you can use *tall* or *ucut* instead of *sin*, so *in fer tall* 'the man there/yonder man' as opposed to the sense of closeness expressed by *in fer so* 'this man' (compare the American colloquialism 'this here man') – see GOI §475(c).

VII. THE VERB

Now this is where it really gets interesting: the verb. It is the bane of many a student's (and scholar's) existence. While the verbal system in Old Irish is complicated, it is actually fairly regulated (and regular), which is good news, because this means that you too can learn it – if you put in time and effort (this means practicing, and reading this section a lot. Sorry). So it is high time to separate the women from the girls and the men from the boys, beginning with some general concepts. Do yourself proud.

VII.a. General
In Old Irish, the verb is **conjugated**. This means that it takes different forms for the different persons. There are 6 persons in total: first person singular (I), second person singular (you), third person singular (used for he, she and it); first person plural (we), second person plural (you) and third person plural (they).

If the subject of the verb is a noun in the singular, you use the third person singular (he/she/it), e.g. *beirid in fer*, 'the man carries'; if the subject of the verb stands in either dual or plural, you use the third person plural, e.g. *mórait fir macc*, 'men praise a boy' or *mórait dá macc fer* 'two boys praise a man'. The reason why you find the plural form with the dual is very simple: the verb has no dual form. The dual is found only with nouns in Old Irish.

In cases where the verb is used in conjunction with a vocative, you use the second person singular or plural, since you are addressing someone (and I apologize for the atrocious sentences I am about to write): *a maicc, in mórai daltae?* 'o son, do you (sg.) praise a fosterling?' and *a maccu, glantae tech* 'o boys, you (pl.) clean a house'.

Active, passive and deponent voice
Distinction is made between active verbal forms, passive verbal forms and deponent verbal forms.

Sentences with **active** verbal forms in them are sentences in which the **subject** of the sentence **performs the action** described in the verb ('the man sees', 'the dog kills' etc., where 'the man' and 'the dog', the two subjects, actively do the seeing and the killing).

In sentences with **passive** verbal forms, the **subject undergoes the action** described by the verb, e.g. 'the man is beaten', 'the dog is killed' – here the man and the dog are (rather unfortunately for them) on the receiving end.

Deponent verbal forms are (by the time Old Irish comes around) basically verbs that look passive in form, but have an active meaning.

Dependent and independent verbal forms

In Old Irish, each verb has two forms for each person in each tense or mood (wow, that sounds complicated. Or something you might bring up at a party to impress people. Then again, maybe not): a **dependent** form and an **independent** form.

You find the dependent form if the verb is preceded by a so-called **conjunct particle**.

Some of the most common conjunct particles are the negative particle *ní* ('not') and the interrogative particle *in* (you find this at the beginning of a question, and you don't have to translate it).

If the verbal form is **not preceded** by a conjunct particle, you find the **independent** form (usually, the independent form is not preceded by anything and just stands at the beginning of a sentence).

Weak verbs and strong verbs

In Old Irish, we distinguish between two kinds of verbs: **weak verbs** and **strong verbs**. Weak verbs are usually very regular and follow a certain pattern; in strong verbs you tend to find irregularities. Weak verbs are often formed from other words, like nouns. Most verbs are weak verbs. The best example of a strong verb in English is probably the verb 'to be.'
Weak verbs generally take an *ā*-subjunctive, *f*-future and *s*-preterite.

Simple and compound verbs

A verb in Old Irish, no matter if it is weak or strong, is either a **simple verb** or a **compound verb**. This means that you can find weak simple verbs, strong simple verbs, weak compound verbs and strong compound verbs.

A simple verb consists only of a verb-part or verbal stem plus ending.
A compound verb consists of any number of preverbs (usually up to four in Old Irish), and a verb-part or verbal stem plus ending.

A **preverb** is a word that is put in front of the verb; it looks exactly like a preposition. I will discuss this in more detail below. An example of a simple verb in English is 'take'. An example of a compound is 'under-take'. An example in Old Irish of a simple verb is *beirid* ('carries'); an Old Irish example of a compound verb is *do-beir* ('gives', 'brings').

I mentioned above that each verb has a dependent and an independent form. **Simple** verbs can take either the **absolute** form (this is the name for the independent form of the verb, which is not preceded by a conjunct particle), or the **conjunct** form (this is the dependent form of the verb, which is preceded by a conjunct particle). The independent form of the **compound** verb is called **deuterotonic**; the dependent form is called **prototonic**. I will get back to these last two terms later.

The five verbal stems
Old Irish verbs can have five different stems that are used to make up the different tenses (e.g. present or past) and moods (indicative, subjunctive or imperative): the present stem, the subjunctive stem, the future stem, the preterite active stem and the preterite passive stem.

(1) The **present stem** is used to make the present indicative, the imperfect indicative and the imperative;

(2) The **subjunctive stem** is used to make the present subjunctive and the past-subjunctive;

(3) The **future stem** is used to make the future and the secondary future (also known as the conditional);

(4) The **preterite active** is used for the preterite (active) and perfect (active) (the perfect is especially in more recent works also referred to as 'augmented preterite');

(5) The **preterite passive** is used for the preterite passive and the perfect passive.

These stems will be discussed in this order below. Now, you may ask yourself: how exactly are these different tenses and moods constructed? Very simple: by adding a specific ending to a specific stem. If you want to put a verb in a secondary future, you take the future stem of that verb and add the secondary ending that goes with it. Sounds easy, doesn't it?

VII.b. The present stem

VII.b.1. The present indicative
(*GOI*: §§546-95; Lehmann: 8, 21-2, 55, 63, 85; McCone: 68-70; Quin: lessons 1-3, 6-10, 13, 14; Stifter: 66,-7,78-9, 90-2, 103-5, 132-5, 151-4; Strachan:34-8, 40-2; Tigges: 27-31, 41-4, 151-9)

The present indicative is your regular every-day present tense: I walk, I see, I fall, etc. But before we can look at the actual patterns of the present tense of the Old Irish verb, you need to know that in Old Irish, based on certain characteristics, verbs are placed in different groups.

In the different grammars that are out there, there are different designations for these groups. This can become awfully confusing. Please note that in this book, I will either adhere to Thurneysen's classification in *GOI* since that is the one most widely used, or I will give a more general description (as in 'verbs of the *marbaid*-type'). This is the classification of the verbs in groups found in the six different grammars I refer to under each heading:

Weak verbs (the marbaid- and léicid-group):
GOI: AI (*marbaid*-group) and AII (*léicid*-group)
Lehmann: refers to verbs as weak verbs
McCone: W1 (*marbaid*-group) and W2 (*léicid*-group)
Quin: does not give specific designations
Stifter: W1 (*marbaid*-group) and W2 (*léicid*-group)
Strachan: B(1) (*marbaid*-type) and B(2) (*léicid*-type)
Tigges: uses different descriptions but refers to   Thurneysen's
            system in *GOI*

Strong verbs (beirid-group, gaibid-group, benaid-group):
GOI: BI (*beirid*-group), BII (*gaibid*-group), BIV (*benaid*-group)[22]
Lehmann: refers to verbs as strong verbs; note: this book only gives
            the pattern for the *beirid*-group and the   deponents   of   the
            gaibid-group as far as strong verbs are considered
McCone: S1 (*beirid*-group), S2 (*gaibid*-group), S3 (*benaid*-group)
Quin: does not give specific designations
Stifter: S1 (*beirid*-group), S2 (*gaibid*-group), S3 (*benaid*-group)
Strachan: A(1) (*beirid*-group), A(3) (*gaibid*-group), A(2) (*benaid* group)
Tigges: uses different descriptions but refers to   Thurneysen's
            system in *GOI*

---

[22] Thurneysen also distinguishes verbs belonging to a BIII and BV class, but as these are relatively rare, these will not be discussed here.

Hiatus verbs

GOI:	AIII
Lehmann:	not discussed
McCone:	H1 (stem ends in *a*-), H2 (stem ends in *i*-), H3 (stem ends in other vowel)
Quin:	not discussed
Stifter:	H1 (stem ends in *a*-), H2 (stem ends in *i*-), H3 (stem ends in other vowel)
Strachan:	not discussed
Tigges:	not discussed

The present indicative active of weak simple verbs

(*GOI*: §§546, 555-7; Lehmann: 8, 21, 55; McCone: 68-70; Quin: lessons 1, 2; Stifter: 66-7; Strachan:37-8; Tigges: 27-31, 41 (full paradigm), 153)

There are two main types of weak verbs. Firstly, there are weak verbs of which **the stem** (also called the root) **ends in a neutral** (also called 'broad') **consonant or consonant group** – these verbs are also called "long a" or *ā*-verbs. Then, there are weak verbs of which **the stem ends in a palatal** (or 'slender') **consonant or consonant group** – these verbs are also called "long i" or *ī*-verbs.

PLEASE NOTE: this refers to the final consonant **of the stem/root**, NOT the final consonant of the word! Take for example the verbal form *marbaid*, 'he/she kills'. The verb *marbaid* is a weak *ā*-verb with a stem ending in a neutral consonant group, because the stem, *marb*-, ends in a neutral consonant group. Once again: DO NOT look at the last consonant of the word, because that one is actually a palatal one here: *marb-ai**d***.

Now, let's say you are reading a text and, oh horror, you encounter a verbal form. How exactly do you know what the stem of this verb is? It is really simple: you chop off the ending and voilà: you have found the stem.

This is true for all verbal forms, but for now let's imagine we are dealing with a present indicative of a weak simple verb. If you do not know which part of the word the ending is, look in the schedule below. In the case of the verbal form *marbaid*, for example, *-aid* is the ending, and *marb*- is therefore the stem; if you find the form *léiciu*, you can see from the table below that *–iu* is the ending, and therefore *léic*- is the stem. In order to supply the other persons of the present indicative, all you have to do is replace the ending you have just removed with one of the endings below:

	Absolute	**Conjunct**	
Sg. 1.	-(a)im, -(i)u	-(a)im, -(i)u	'I'
Sg. 2.	-(a)i	-(a)i	'you'
Sg. 3.	-(a)id	-a or –i	'he/she/it'
Pl. 1.	-m(a)i	-am or –em	'we'
Pl. 2.	-th(a)e	-(a)id	'you'
Pl. 3.	-(a)it	-at or -et	'they'

For verbs like *marbaid*, i.e. the weak *ā*-verbs that have a root in a neutral consonant (group), remember to stick in the *a* in the endings where applicable, and use the forms in –*a*, -*am* or –*at*. Likewise, for the weak *ī*-verbs with a root ending in a palatal consonant (group) like *léicid*, use the *i*-glide for the first person singular, leave out the (*a*) from the list above and use the –*i*, -*em* and –*et* endings in 3sg., 1 and 3 pl.

A note: in *DIL*, as well as in most other textual editions, entries for verbs are listed in the third person singular present indicative absolute (or deuterotonic – we will get to that later, so do not worry for now – so you would find *glanaid, marbaid, léicid* etc.).

And now you have all the basics. Let's try it out. If you want to say 'we allow', and you know you need the present stem of the verb *léicid*, you remove the ending –*id*. This leaves you with the stem; then you stick on the ending for 1 pl. –*mi*. Result: *léicmi* – which is the correct answer.

The present indicative passive of weak simple verbs
(*GOI*: §§577, 579; Lehmann: 55; McCone: 103-5; Quin: lesson 13; Stifter: 154; Strachan: 37-8; Tigges: 29, 41, 153)

We have seen the regular forms of the present indicative of the weak simple verb, in which the subject performs the action (I go, he kills etc.). This is also called the active voice. But almost every verb also has a passive form. The most important thing to remember is this:

> In passive verbal forms, the subject **undergoes** the action (this is expressed in English by using the verb to be).

An example:
I bite – active voice: the subject, I, is the person doing the biting;
I am bitten – passive voice: the subject, I, is the person undergoing the biting – ouch!

Now the thing is, in Old Irish, there is a special passive form of the verb, but there are only two persons in the verb that have this special form! These are the **3 sg.** and the **3 pl.** Usually, the passive is easily identifiable by the use of the letter '*r*' in the ending. Here are the basic forms for the weak verbs:

	Absolute	**Conjunct**
Sg. 3.	*-th(a)ir*	*-thar/-ther*
Pl. 3.	*-t(a)ir*	*-tar/-ter*

If you want to put a verb in the passive, you take the stem and add the appropriate ending, so if you want to say 'he is killed', and you know that the verb for 'to kill' is *marbaid*, you take the stem – which you now know is *marb-* – and add the ending you need, which is the third person singular absolute passive. The result of that is of course *marbthair*. If you want to say 'they are not allowed', you first grab the stem of *léicid*, which is *léic*, and then add the ending. In this case, the verbal form will follow the word *ní* 'not', which is a conjunct particle. You therefore need the conjunct ending for 3 pl. *–ter*, giving you *léicter* (you use *–ter* rather than *–tar* here because the *c* in *léic* is palatal). Great!

But how do you express the first and second persons singular and plural (I, you, we, you); how do you say 'I am allowed' or 'you are killed'? The way this is done in Old Irish is by using the dependent form of the **third person singular passive plus an infixed pronoun of the person you need** (the infixed pronoun is explained in detail in V.b. above). Note that I said 'dependent form' (i.e. the conjunct form or prototonic form), because remember: you need to insert the infixed pronoun somewhere. If there are no conjunct particles present to tack the infixed pronoun onto, you need to use the particle *no*. If we want to make a paradigm expressing 'x is killed', for example, you need to use the particle *no* plus the conjunct form 3sg. passive (*–marbthar*) plus the infixed pronoun, and this is what you get:

nom-marbthar	'I am killed' (lit. 'one kills me')
not-marbthar	'you are killed' (lit. 'one kills you')
marbthair	'he/she/it is killed' (special form)
non-marbthar	'we are killed' (lit. 'one kills us' – note that here you find the conjunct form of the 3 sg., and not the 3 pl., as you might have expected)
nob-marbthar	'you (pl.) are killed' (lit. 'one kills you' – again with 3 sg. passive)
marbtar	'they are killed' (special form)

The **agent** of the verb, in other words, the person who performs the action that the subject undergoes, is expressed in English by the preposition 'by' (in the sentence 'the dog is killed **by the man**', the subject, 'the dog', undergoes the action (the killing, in this case), and the agent, that is to say, the person who does the killing, is 'the man'). In Old Irish, the agent is usually expressed by using the preposition *la*, e.g. *marbtair **lasin fer**, 'they are killed **by the man**'.

Sometimes you find **intransitive verbs** in the passive. Intransitive verbs are verbs that do not take a direct object (like in English: I crawl). The opposite of intransitive verbs are **transitive** verbs, which do take a direct object (I see a horse, I drink a pint of Guinness etc.). When **intransitive verbs** are found in the **passive**, it is probably easiest to translate them in an **impersonal sense** as well (some examples of impersonal sentences: someone goes, one shouts, etc.). The most common passive intransitive verb form is probably *tíagair*, the passive of the verb *téit*. You can translate this literally with 'there is a going', or 'messengers are sent' (which is not as crazy-sounding as 'there is a going').

Weak deponent verbs
(*GOI*: §§ 569-76; Lehmann: -, but see pp. 21-2, 124; McCone: 111-2; Quin: lesson 3; Stifter: 151-2; Strachan: 41-2; Tigges: 154)

Those of you who have studied Latin might have heard of deponent verbs already, as many of them can be found in Latin, for example *sequitur*, 'he follows'. I shall not go into much detail; just remember that deponents are basically a group of verbs with their own set of endings. The most distinguishing feature for deponent verbs in Old Irish is that it **typically has the letter -r as the last letter in its endings** (with the exception of a few instances mentioned in the next paragraph).

By the Old Irish period, deponents were a dying breed. At the time that we are looking at, there are no longer special deponent forms for all the different tenses and in some cases (second person plural absolute and conjunct in both groups of weak deponent verbs and the first person singular absolute in weak deponent verbs with a stem ending in a slender consonant group) it **never** has special deponent endings. In those cases, the weak deponent verb takes the endings we have seen for the verb types like *marbaid* and *léicid* (those endings are officially called active endings).

The weak deponent verbs are divided into two groups: deponent verbs of which the end of the stem is neutral or broad (like in *labr-aithir* 'speaks') and those of which the stem ends in a palatal or slender consonant group (like in *foilsig-idir* 'reveals'). Note that in the second group, the last two letters of the root are usually –*ig.*

A. Stems ending in a **neutral consonant** (e.g. *labraithir* 'speaks', *comalnaithir*, 'fulfills, discharges') have the following pattern:

		Absolute	**Conjunct**
Sg.	1.	*-ur*	*-ur*
	2.	*-(a)ither*	*-(a)ither*
	3.	*-(a)ithir*	*-athar*
Pl.	1.	*-(a)immir*	*-ammar*
	2.	*-th(a)e*	*-(a)id*
	3.	*-(a)itir*	*-atar*

B. Stems ending in a **palatal consonant** (e.g. *foilsigidir* 'reveals', *suidigidir* 'places'; also, I just found the fantastic verbs *aininnracaigidir* 'regards as unworthy', *aidilccnigidir* 'needs, wants' – these final two I have not yet seen in any text I have translated as far as I remember, but I can't wait) follow this pattern:

		Absolute	**Conjunct**
Sg.	1.	*-im / -iur*	*-ur*
	2.	*-ther*	*-ther*
	3.	*-idir*	*-edar*
Pl.	1.	*-mir*	*-mer*
	2.	*-the*	*-id*
	3.	*-itir*	*-etar*

Again, if you wish to conjugate other weak deponents, and you have figured out to which type they belong (the *labraithir*-type or the *foilsigidir*-type), you just have to chop off the ending and replace it with the one you want.

Example: say you want to say 'they do not place' using the verb *suidigidir.* The two things you need to do first: (1) look at the person you need. The form 'they' is the third person plural; (2) Since you need to use the word *ní* 'not' – which is a conjunct particle – you need the conjunct form of the verb. The ending you need, as you can see above, is –*etar.* Now that you know that, all you need to do is cut off the ending and replace it. The ending of the verb is –*idir* as you can see in the list above. From the facts that the ending is –*idir* and that the stem ends in –*ig,* you can say that this verb belongs to the *foilsigidir*-group. You are left with *suidig-.* Then add the ending and presto, you have the correct answer: *ní suidigetar.*

Another example: let's say you want to put *comalnaithir* in the first person plural absolute, giving you 'we fulfill'. The ending in the word *comalnaithir* is *–aithir*, so you remove that and you are left with *comaln-* (you can see that this does not belong to the *foilsigidir*-group since there is no *-ig* in sight). Then, you tack on *–aimmir* (the *a* is there because the stem ends in a neutral consonant group), and you end up with *comalnaimmir*. See – easy.

It is important to bear in mind that just like active verbs, deponent verbs can also be made passive by adding the passive endings for 3 sg. and 3 pl. to the stem. The endings are the same as given above, namely:

		Absolute	**Conjunct**
Sg.	3.	*-th(a)ir*	*-thar/ -ther*
Pl.	3.	*-t(a)ir*	*-tar/ -ter*

So for example, the third person singular present indicative passive absolute of *foilsigidir* 'he/she/it reveals' is *foilsig**thir*** 'he/she/it is revealed').

Present indicative active of strong verbs
(*GOI*: §§548-54, 558-68, 591-5; Lehmann: 8, 21-2; McCone: 68-70; Quin: lessons 6-8; Stifter:90-2, 103-5; Strachan: 35-6; Tigges: 29-30, 42, 156 ff.)

So far, we have only looked at *weak verbs*. We have seen that the weak verbs can be divided into two groups: one group consists of verbs of which the final consonant (group) of the stem (or root) is neutral or broad, such as *marbaid*. The other group consists of verbs of which the final consonant (group) of the stem ends in a palatal or slender consonant, such as *léicid*. Moreover, we have also seen weak deponent verbs that can basically be divided along the same lines: one kind has a root ending in a neutral or broad consonant (group), like *labraithir* and *comalnaithir*; one kind has a root ending in a palatal or slender consonant, like *foilisigidir* and *suidigidir*.

There is also a second group of verbs: strong verbs. Strong verbs are usually much older than weak verbs and they tend to be more irregular. An example of a strong verb in English is the verb 'to be'. Now, let us look at the three main types of strong verbs in Old Irish. There are two more groups that are very rare, and therefore they are not considered in detail here.

By the way, this may be handy to know: you can distinguish a weak verb from a strong verb in the present indicative by looking at the third person singular conjunct active. Weak verbs end in a vowel (e.g. *ní marba*, *ní léici*);

98

strong verbs in the third person singular conjunct look like the verbal stem (*ní beir, ní gaib*).

The first type of strong verb: *beirid*-group

Present indicative active
(*GOI*: §§ 548, 558, 591-2; Lehmann: 8, 21, 85; McCone: 68-70; Quin: lesson 6; Stifter: 90-2; Strachan: 35; Tigges: 29, 42, 156)

The main characteristic about the verbs belonging to this group is that the **final consonant (group) of the stem is sometimes slender (=palatal) and sometimes broad (=neutral)**. There is a pattern to this: the stem in the first person singular, first person plural and third person plural ends in a neutral consonant; the stem ends in a palatal consonant in the second person singular, the third person singular and the second person plural.[23]

With the exception of a few forms (namely the conjunct form of the first person singular, the conjunct form of the second person singular and the conjunct form of the third person singular) the endings look pretty much the same as the endings that we have already seen - you find the endings that look like those of the *marbaid* group if the final consonant of the verbal stem is neutral or broad, and you will find the endings that look like those of the *léicid* group if the final consonant of the verbal stem is palatal.

Here is the pattern for the verb *beirid*:[24]

Ending	Absolute	Conjunct
Sg. 1.	-*u*; note in example below that the *e* of the stem has become an *i*	none, but *u* inserted before final consonant (group)

---

[23] If you know Latin, the following may help you remember the Irish pattern (I know this sounds really strange, but I know it helped me a lot, so use it or not as you see fit): in Latin, the present indicative of the verb 'to be', *esse*, has the paradigm: *sum* ('I am'), *es* ('you are'), *est* ('he/she/it is'), *sumus* ('we are'), *estis* ('you are'), *sunt* ('they are'). The forms that begin in *su-* correspond to the Irish neutral forms in the *beirid*-pattern, the forms beginning in *e-* correspond to the Irish palatal forms.

[24] This pattern is also followed by one of the two other groups of strong verbs that are not treated here – these verbs belong to a group that Thurneysen refers to as BIII; the presten stem of these verbs ends in –*ng* or –*nd*; an example is the verb *toingid* 'swears', with stem *toing-*; see *GOI* §550.

	2.	*-i*; again, note that the *e* of the stem has changed	none; ending *-i* is just chopped off (the *e* of the stem is still *i*) into an *i*
	3.	*-id*	none; *-id* is just chopped off
Pl.	1.	*-mai*	*-am*
	2.	*-the*	*-id*
	3.	*-ait*	*-at*

Now, the forms of the verb *beirid*:

		Absolute	Conjunct	Translation	Quality of final consonant of verbal stem
Sg.	1.	*biru*	(*ní*) *biur*	I carry	neutral
	2.	*biri*	(*ní*) *bir*	you carry	palatal
	3.	*beirid*	(*ní*) *beir*	he/she/it carries	palatal
Pl.	1.	*bermai*	(*ní*) *beram*	we carry	neutral
	2.	*beirthe*	(*ní*) *beirid*	you carry	palatal
	3.	*berait*	(*ní*) *berat*	they carry	neutral

That is not too bad, now is it? See, Old Irish is not as difficult as you might think; there is usually a very organized method to the madness! Let us go on to the passive form of this group of verbs.

Present indicative passive
(*GOI*: §§540, 577ff.; Lehmann: 55; McCone: 68-70; Quin: lesson 13; Stifter: 154; Strachan: 35; Tigges: 32-3, 156)

The regular form of the passive is exactly the same as the pattern found for the verbs in the *marbaid-* and *léicid-*group, so 3 sg. absolute: *-thair*; conjunct – *thar*; and 3 pl. absolute: *-tair*, conjunct *-tar*. But note that in the 3 sg. in some of the strong verbs in this group, the *-th-* is dropped in 3 sg. (like *beirid*, which has pass. sg. *berair* 'he/she/it is carried').

The second type of strong verb: *gaibid*-group
(*GOI*: §§549, 554, 593; Lehmann: - ; McCone: 68-70; Quin: lesson 7; Stifter: 103, 105; Strachan: 36; Tigges: 30, 42, 157-8)

All verbs in this group have a verbal root **ending in a palatal consonant (group)** for all persons (so no fluctuations here): *gaib-id, gair-id* etc. Apart from the third person singular conjunct, which has no ending (i.e., has nothing added to the stem), the endings are the same as we have already seen for the verbs of the *léicid* group:

Active

The endings for active verbal forms are:

		Absolute	Conjunct
Sg.	1.	*-iu/-im*	*-iu/-im*
	2.	*-i*	*-i*
	3.	*-id*	no ending
Pl.	1.	*-mi*	*-em*
	2.	*-the*	*-id*
	3.	*-it*	*-et*

Example:

		Absolute	Conjunct	Translation
Sg.	1.	*gaibiu/gaibim*	*(ní) gaibiu/gaibim*	I seize
	2.	*gaibi*	*(ní) gaibi*	you seize
	3.	*gaibid*	*(ní) gaib*	he/she/it seizes
Pl.	1.	*gaibmi*	*(ní) gaibem*	we seize
	2.	*gaibthe*	*(ní) gaibid*	you seize
	3.	*gaibit*	*(ní) gaibet*	they seize

Passive

(*GOI*: no paradigm given, cp. §§ 577 ff.; Lehmann: 55; McCone: 103; Quin: lesson 13; Stifter: 154; Strachan: 37; Tigges: 33, 157-8)

The forms used for the passive are:

		Absolute	Conjunct
Sg	3.	*-thir*	*-ther*
Pl.	3.	*-tir*	*-ter*

Examples: *gaib**thir*** 'he is seized'; *ní gaib**ther*** 'he is not seized'; *gaib**tir*** 'they are seized', *ní gaib**ter*** 'they are not seized'

Deponent

(*GOI*: §§540, 569-76; Lehmann: 21-2, 55; McCone: 111-6; Quin: lesson 7; Stifter: 153; Strachan: 40-1; Tigges: 45)

Virtually all strong deponent verbs belong in this group of strong verbs.[25]

---

[25] There are two verbs, *ro-cluinethar* 'hears' and *ro-finnadar* 'finds out', that actually belong to the *benaid*-group (Stifter: 153). They lose the particle *ro* if they stand in dependent position, so *ro-cluiniur* 'I hear', *ní cluiniur* 'I do not hear'. The endings of

They all have a verbal root ending in a palatal consonant (group). As one of the most common verbs in this group is *midithir* 'judges', I will refer to this group as the *midithir*-group. The endings of the *midithir*-group look very much like the endings of the *labraithir*-group - but of course palatal and without the *a*. Allow me to demonstrate:

		Endings *labraithir*-group		Endings *midithir*-group	
		Absolute	**Conjunct**	**Absolute**	**Conjunct**
Sg.	1.	*-ur*	*-ur*	*-iur*	*-iur*
	2.	*-(a)ither*	*-(a)ither*	*-ther*	*-ther*
	3.	*-(a)ithir*	*-athar*	*-ithir*	*-athar*
Pl.	1.	*-(a)immir*	*-ammar*	*-immir*	*-emmar*
	2.	*-th(a)e*	*-(a)id*	*-the*	*-id*
	3.	*-(a)itir*	*-atar*	*-itir*	*-etar*

Here is the full pattern for *midithir*, with stem *mid-*:

		Absolute	**Conjunct**	**Translation**
Sg.	1.	*midiur*	*(ni) midiur*	I judge
	2.	**mitter**	**(ni) mitter**	You judge
	3.	*midithir*	*(ni) midethar*	He/She/It judges
Pl.	1.	*midimmir*	*(ni) midemmar*	We judge
	2.	**mitte**	*(ni) midid*	You judge
	3.	*miditir*	*(ni) midetar*	They judge

Now I am sure you have noticed some forms that might look strange at first - especially since I have highlighted them: the absolute and conjunct forms of the second person singular and the absolute form of the second person plural (and note the 'regular' active ending of the second person plural!). Instead of seeing the letter *d*, which you might expect, you find the letter *t*. What has happened? Let us look at these forms in more detail.

The second person singular absolute and conjunct
The ending you would expect in both cases is *-ther*. And that is actually the ending that you find here. Except two things happened. Let us reconstruct it. You first take the stem, which is *mid-*, and then you add the ending *-ther*. The outcome is then **mid-ther*. Now the letters *t* and *d* are homorganic consonants, so you get **delenition** (and we have already seen delenition before so you should all know what I am talking about! If not, you can find

---

ro-*cluinethar* look like those of *midithir* above; for those of ro-*finnadar*, only 3 sg., 1pl. and 3 pl. have been attested: 3 sg. ro-*finnadar*, *-finnadar*; 1 pl. ro-*finnammar*, -*finnammar*; 3 pl. ro-*finnatar*, *-finnatar*.

it in the discussion on lenition way back in the first chapter on general terms). Then you are left with *mid-ter. Now if a letter *d* is followed by the letter *t*, as is the case here (or if it is preceded by the letter *s*, but that is not important right now), something else happens that is called **devoicing** which makes the letter *d* change into the letter *t*. The outcome of that is what we see above: *mitter, (ní) mitter.*

The second person plural absolute

What happens here is exactly the same! You add the ending *-the* to the stem *mid-*: what you get is *mid-the*. Then you get delenition and, because the letter *d* is followed by the letter *t*, devoicing of the *d* to *t* and voilà: the outcome is *mitte* - there is nothing irregular about it.

For those interested as to why this is called *devoicing*:
The letters *d* and *t* (as well as the letters *g* and *c* and *b* and *p*) are sometimes called *stops*. When you pronounce a stop, it closes the vocal tract so that it stops the airflow – in other words, the sound only comes out once. You cannot continuously pronounce the sound made by these letters for extended periods of time, in contrast to for example the letter *l* - you can hold that one for a long time. Now, the stops *d, g* and *b* are called voiced stops, because when you pronounce them, you are using your vocal chords. The stops *t, c* and *p* are called voiceless stops, because (you guessed it!) when you pronounce them you do NOT use your vocal chords. If the voiced stop *d* is devoiced, you get its voiceless equivalent *t*; *g* becomes *c* (sounds like *k*) and *b* becomes *p*.

The third type of strong verb: *benaid*-group

(*GOI*: §§551, 553-4, 568, 594; Lehmann:- ; McCone: 68-70; Quin: lesson 8; Stifter:104; Strachan: 35-6; Tigges: 30, 42, 159)

This group of strong verbs all have a **stem or root ending in a neutral (=broad) letter *n*** in the present stem: *ben-aid, cren-aid,* etc.[26]

Apart from the third person singular conjunct, the endings are basically the same as those you find in the *marbaid*-group. But be careful: because the stems of the verbs in this group always ends in the letter *-n*, you get delenition in the second person plural absolute:

---

[26] The final group of strong verbs treated in *GOI*, Thurneysen's B V, is apparently inflected like the B IV verbs, but the preceding vowel is not neutral, e.g. *ara-chrin* 'decays', *do-lin* 'flows'.

Active

		Absolute	Conjunct	Translation
Sg.	1.	*benaim*	*(ní) benaim*	I strike
	2.	*benai*	*(ní) benai*	You strike
	3.	*benaid*	*(ní) ben*	He/she strikes
Pl.	1.	*benmai*	*(ní) benam*	We strike
	2.	*ben**tae***	*(ní) benaid*	You strike
	3.	*benait*	*(ní) benat*	They strike

If you are an observant reader, you may have noticed that I wrote that the stem of these verbs ends in the letter *n* in the present stem – and for good reason! The ***n* is not found in the other stems**, which can make it difficult to look up in a dictionary. More about this later, when we get to the other verbal stems.

Passive
(*GOI*: §§553-4, 594; Lehmann: - ; McCone: 103; Quin: lesson 13; Stifter:154; Strachan: 35-6; Tigges: 32-3, 71, 151 ff.)

The special passive forms for the strong verbs of the *benaid*-group look exactly like those for the *marbaid*-type weak verbs, except that the *-th-* is omitted in the singular:

		Absolute	Conjunct	Example	Translation
Sg.	3.	*-air*	*-ar*	*benair*	he/she/it is struck
				ní benar	he/she/it is not struck
Pl.	3	*-tair*	*-tar*	*bentair*	they are struck
				ní bentar	they are not struck

Hiatus verbs
(*GOI*: §§547, 589-90; Lehmann: - ; McCone: 67-8; Quin: - ; Stifter: 132; Strachan: - ; Tigges: -)[27]

Apart from the weak and strong verbs, there is also a class called hiatus verbs. As you all know by know, this refers to the fact that two adjoining vowels are pronounced separately. In this case, the first vowel is the final letter of the stem, and the second vowel is the first vowel of the ending, as in *gníid*, 'does, makes' with stem *gni-* and ending *–id*. In other words, the stem of the hiatus verbs **ends in a vowel**.

---

[27] This section is based on the discussions in *GOI*, McCone and Stifter.

Although there are not that many hiatus verbs, some of them are very common and important, like *at-tá* and *biid*, 'is' and 'is usually' (see below section IX), *ad-cí* 'sees', *gniid* 'does, makes', *do-gní* 'does, makes'. There are three groups of hiatus verbs.[28] Of the first group, the final vowel of the stem is *–a/-á* (e.g. *at-tá* 'is' with stem *tá-*). Of the second group, the final stem vowel is *–i/-í* (e.g. *cïid* 'weeps', stem *ci-*); the third group, surprise, has a stem ending in a vowel other than *–a* or *–i* (so *e, o* or *u*, e.g. *srëid* 'throws', *foïd* 'sleeps with', *bruïd* 'breaks'). Especially this third group is found rarely, and we don't have a complete paradigm for it, but the pattern for the present of the hiatus verbs is very similar for the three classes:

Basic pattern of the endings in the present indicative active of the hiatus verbs

		Absolute	Conjunct
Sg.	1.	*–u, (a)im*	*–u, -(a)im*
	2.	*–i*	*–i*
	3.	*–id*	no ending (root vowel)
Pl.	1.	*–m(a)i*	*–am*
	2.	unattested[29]	*–id*
	3.	*–(a)it*	*–at*

You just add these endings to the root vowels of each group, with the following results. The verbs used in the table below are *snaïd* 'swims', *baïd* 'dies' *at-tá* 'is', *cïid* 'weeps', *liïd* 'accuses', *biïd* 'is usually', *gniid* 'does, makes', *sóïd* 'turns', *srëid* 'throws', *bruïd* 'breaks'. Notice how similar the endings are:

		Group 1		Group 2		Group 3	
		Absolute	Conjunct	Absolute	Conjunct	Absolute	Conjunct
Sg.	1.	**snau*	*-táu, -tó*	*bíu, líim*	*-gníu*	**sréu*	**-sou, *-sréu*
	2.	**snai*	*-tái*	*cíi*	*-gní*	**soi*	**-brui*
	3.	*snaid*	*-tá, -ba*	*cïid*	*-gní*	*soid*	*-soí,*[30] **-brui, *-sré*
Pl.	1.	**snami?*	*-baam*	*limmi*	*-gniam*	**srémi*	**-soam, *-bruam*
	2.	**snaithi?*	*-taid*	**cíthi?*	*-gniid*	**sothi?*	**-sréid, *-bruid*
	3.	*snait*	*-baat*	*cïit, líit*	*-gniat*	*so(a)it*	*-soat, *sréat*

---

[28] Thurneysen treats these as one group in *GOI* §547, but see §589 and §644, where he does list hiatus verbs ending in *–i, -a* and *-o*.

[29] One would perhaps expect an ending like *–th(a)e* here.

[30] Verbs with a stem ending in *-o* or *-u* have an ending *–oí, -uí*, as in *–foí, as-luí*, but the verb *scëid* 'vomits' with stem in *-é* has the form *–scé* – see Stifter: 134.

Passive of hiatus verbs

These forms are very rare. We have reliable attested forms for the conjunct forms of the second group of hiatus verbs (with stem in *–i*), as well as a form *ráithir* 'is rowed', from the early Old Irish text *Audacht Morainn* 'Morann's Testament' (seventh century), giving us the following endings:

	Absolute	**Conjunct**
Sg. 3.	*-thir* (or *–ithir*)	*-ther* (or *–ither?*)
Pl. 3.	**-tar/ter*	*-ter, *-tar*

Compound verbs

(*GOI*: §§37-8, 543-4; Lehmann: 78-9; McCone: 71-4; Quin: lessons 9-10; Stifter: 77-80, 92; Strachan: -; Tigges: 58-62, 82, 119, 155-6, 158)

Up to now, we have been looking at simple verbs - verbs that only consist of a verbal part and an ending, like Irish *marb-aid* and English *take*. Now, we are going to take a look at a new kind of verb - the compound verb. A compound verb, as I mentioned at the beginning of this chapter, is a verb that in addition to a verbal stem + an ending, consists of any number of preverbs (in Old Irish there can usually be up to four preverbs, but most often there is just one). The preverb, as you may have guessed from its name, stands **before** the verb. It looks exactly like a preposition. Some examples of compound verbs in Old Irish are *do-beir*, 'brings, gives', *do-gní*, 'does', *as-beir* 'says'; some examples in English are *undergo, undertake, forbear*. In other words:

> If you want to turn a simple verb into a compound verb, all you have to do is add preverbs to a simple verb. After these preverbs, you use the **conjunct form** of the (simple) verb.

This means that if you want to make a compound verb out of the simple verb *beirid*, you take a preverb, for example *as* 'out of' (related to Latin '*ex*'), and add the **conjunct ending** of the person that you are looking for. The outcome for the present indicative is as follows:

	Simple verb		**Compound verb**	
	beirid 'carries'		***as-beir*** 'says'	
	Absolute	**Conjunct**		
Sg.1	*biru*	*ní* **biur**	*as-***biur**	I say
2	*biri*	*ní* **bir**	*as-***bir**	you say
3	*beirid*	*ní* **beir**	*as-***beir**	he/she says
Pl. 1	*bermai*	*ní* **beram**	*as-***beram**	we say

106

| 2 | beirthe | *ní* **beirid** | *as-***beirid** | you say |
| 3 | berait | *ní* **berat** | *as-***berat** | they say |

Do you see how the conjunct forms of *beirid* and the forms after the preverb *as* are the same? This means that you will not have to learn a new set of endings because you already know them (or you should – if you don't, stop right here and go learn them pronto)!

The *verbal part* in a compound verb determines whether this compound verb is going to be *strong or weak*: **if the verb part** in the compound verb **is strong** (for example *do-beir*, 'brings, gives' with the verb part coming from the strong verb *beirid*), the whole compound verb will be strong. If the compound verb is made up with a **weak** verb, like *léicid*, you get a **weak compound verb**, like *do-léici* 'lets loose'.

The preverbs themselves are unstressed. In Old Irish, you generally have only **one unstressed particle before the stress** - so whatever comes after the first unstressed particle will be stressed. An example: if you pronounce the word *do-beir*, you put the stress on *beir*, and not on *do*, because *do* is the unstressed preverb.

This means that the stress falls on the *second* element of the compound verb: preverb - **verbal part** - ending. Are you still following me? So if you have to put the stress in for example *do-léicem*, the stress will be on *-léic* (preverb is *do*, verbal part is *-léic*, ending is *-em*).

This is called the **deuterotonic** form of the verb. The word *deuterotonic* contains the Greek word *deúteros*, meaning 'second'. The word deuterotonic actually means 'stress on the second syllable'.

You use the **deuterotonic form of a compound verb** in exactly the same places where you would find the **absolute form of a simple verb** - so if there are **no conjunct particles** before it like *ní* or *in*.

Compare: ***beirid*** *in fer in macc cosin n-insi*, 'the man carries the boy to the island', where *beirid* is **absolute**
do-beir *in fer in macc cosin n-insi*, 'the man brings the boy to the island', where *do-beir* is **deuterotonic**

Now, I hear you ask: what form of a compound verb do you use if you want to say 'the man does not bring the boy to the island' - a form that you use in those same places where you would use the **conjunct** form of a simple verb, like ***ní beir*** *in fer in macc cosin n-insi*, 'the man does not carry the

107

boy to the island'? Excellent question.

We have just seen that you can only have one unstressed particle before the stress. And I have mentioned before that the conjunct particles like *ní* and *in* are unstressed. So what do we do? Simple: because we can only have one unstressed particle before the stress, the stress has to be put in a different place, namely immediately after the conjunct particle. **This means that the stress will now fall on the (first) preverb.** And since the preverb is the first part of the compound verb, as we have seen (**preverb**-verbal part-ending), we call the resulting forms the **prototonic** form of the verb. Prototonic also contains a Greek word - the word *protos* means 'first' (if you have a hard time remembering this, maybe it helps to think of the English word proto-type) - , so **prototonic** means 'stress on the first syllable'.

Good news: the verbal endings themselves remain basically the same in deuterotonic and prototonic forms so you don't have to learn a new set of endings – but in some cases you get syncope.

We are almost there. Before we can look at what the prototonic forms look like, I have to explain one more thing. Because the preverbs in deuterotonic forms were unstressed and stood right before the stressed part, people tended to pronounce them less clearly. This had already started before the Old Irish period.

> As a result of their pronunciation, some of the Old Irish preverbs that you see in the deuterotonic forms have actually changed from their original form. But in the prototonic forms, the stress shifts to the preverb - and in those forms we see the **original form** of the preverb.

The preverb *do*, for example, can come either from *to-* or from *de-*: this is why you get **do-**beir, ní **ta**bair and **do-**gní, ní **dé**nai. Some of the most common preverbs that change are:[31]

Original preverb   **Form in the deuterotonic verbal form**

to-	*do-*	(e.g. *do-beir* 'he brings/gives', *-tabair*)
de-	*do-*	(e.g. *do-gní* 'he does', *-dénai* (from *de+gní*))[32]

---

[31] Stifter has an awesome overview of all of the preverbs and their pretonic (unstressed) forms, on p. 78 of his book. I highly recommend it.

[32] As you know, with compound words, the first letter of the second word is lenited; in this case that is the letter *g*. This lenited *g* disappears and causes compensatory lengthening (for more on compensatory lengthening, see the chapter on the noun under dental stems).

es-	as-	(e.g. *as-beir* 'he says', *-epir* (from *es+beir*))[33]
con-	co-, cum-	(e.g. *con-icc*, 'he is able', *-cumaic*, *con-tuili*
	con-	'sleeps', *-cotlai*)

Now, let's see what the prototonic forms of the compound verb *do-beir* look like when compared with the simple verb *beirid*:

		Simple verb		Compound verb	
		Absolute	**Conjunct**	**Deuterotonic**	**Prototonic**
Sg.	1.	*biru*	*ní* **biur**	*do-***biur**	*ní ta***bur**
	2.	*biri*	*ní* **bir**	*do-***bir**	*ní ta***bair**
	3.	*beirid*	*ní* **beir**	*do-***beir**	*ní ta***bair**
Pl.	1.	*bermai*	*ní* **beram**	*do-***beram**	*ní tai***brem**
	2.	*beirthe*	*ní* **beirid**	*do-***beirid**	*ní tai***brid**
	3.	*berait*	*ní* **berat**	*do-***berat**	*ní tai***bret**

Once again, do you see that the forms in bold print are (basically) the same? See, isn't it easier than you thought? As you can see, you find syncope in the **prototonic forms in the plural** (*ní taibrem, ní taibrid* and *ní taibret*): *-taibrem* is the result of syncope of **to-ber-am*. The vowel in the second syllable (the letter *e* in *-ber-*) is taken out. Because the vowel *e* is a palatal vowel, the remaining consonant group will be made palatal. Likewise, *-taibrid* is the result of syncope of **to-ber-id* and *-taibret* is the result from syncope of **to-ber-at*.

Hopefully you realize that what makes all the difference between the deuterotonic and the prototonic forms is where the stress falls. With the information I just gave you, you now should be able to turn almost any simple verb into a compound verb; and as long as you know what the conjunct forms of the simple verb look like, you should be able to reconstruct the forms for the deuterotonic and the prototonic! The only thing that might be a little difficult is predicting what the preverb does if it changes from deuterotonic into prototonic, or, to put it differently, what the original preverb looked like. But in practice, that is not really a big problem, since you will usually be translating from Old Irish into English or another language, and not the other way around.

---

[33] Remember in the discussion on the devoicing of *d* in the verbal forms *mitter* and *mitte* in the strong deponents above – I mentioned there that after the letter *s* you could also have devoicing; that is the case here.

VII.b.2. Imperfect indicative
(*GOI*: §§580-2; Lehmann: 21-2, 55 101; McCone: 82-3, 106, 111-12; Quin: lesson 16; Stifter: 242-3; Strachan: 39, 40, 43; Tigges: 107, 111)

Finally we can move on to the imperfect indicative! The imperfect indicative is a tense set in the past, and it is used to describe a **repeated or continuous action in the past**. The best way to translate this into English is by using 'used to,' e.g. 'he used to go to school every day'. First, let me give you some general information. As you know, there are five verb stems in Old Irish. There is the present stem (this is the stem that we have been looking at so far), the subjunctive stem, the future stem, the preterite active stem and the preterite passive stem.

Why am I telling you all this again? Well, because the endings that are used for the imperfect indicative are also used to form the past subjunctive and the secondary future. These endings are sometimes also called **secondary endings**, because they are used to form the secondary (or past) tense of a certain stem.

Now, how do you put a verb in the imperfect indicative? It is very simple. You take the present stem of the verb, e.g. *marb-* or *léic-*, and add the special secondary endings that you can find below. This process will be **exactly the same** for the past subjunctive and the secondary future. In each case, you only have to add the secondary endings to the relevant stem (i.e. if you want to put something in the past subjunctive, you take the subjunctive stem and add the ending you need). Now, what do these endings look like? Like this:

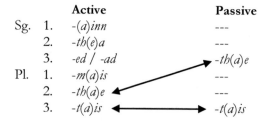

		Active	**Passive**
Sg.	1.	-(*a*)*inn*	---
	2.	-*th*(*e*)*a*	---
	3.	-*ed* / -*ad*	-*th*(*a*)*e*
Pl.	1.	-*m*(*a*)*is*	---
	2.	-*th*(*a*)*e*	---
	3.	-*t*(*a*)*is*	-*t*(*a*)*is*

Note that the **passive** endings **do not contain the letter *r*** as you might expect; also note that the ending for the passive singular looks identical to the ending for the second person plural and that the passive plural ending looks identical to the ending for the third person plural (I have marked this in the table above). Usually this is not a problem – you can figure out which of the two it is from the context. And remember: if a form is **followed by a direct object**, it cannot be passive!

There are three important things you should remember about the imperfect indicative:

1. The imperfect indicative has **NO absolute forms**. This means that you will always find a conjunct particle before a simple verb in the imperfect indicative. If there is no conjunct particle there, the particle *no* is used. For compound verbs, you just add the endings to the verb stem. An example:

Simple verb *beirid*   **Compound verb *do-beir***

no berainn	*ní berainn*	*do-beirinn*	*ní taibrinn*
I used to carry	I didn't use to carry	I used to bring	I didn't use to bring

2. I am sure you will be delighted to know that there are **NO special deponent forms** for the imperfect indicative. Instead, you take the present stem of the deponent verb (*labr-*, *foilsig-*) and add the endings we have seen above. Remember to use the particle *no* if there is nothing else present! For example:

no labrad	*ní foilsigmis*	*no suidigthe*	*ní foilsigtis*
'he used to speak'	'we didn't use to reveal'	'you used to place' or 'it used to be placed'	'they did not use to reveal' or 'they did not use to be revealed'

3. It has been pointed out to me that the verbs from the *beirid*-group **do not have a fluctuating root** (that is, a root that sometimes ends in a neutral consonant and sometimes in a palatal consonant) in the imperfect indicative like they do in the present indicative. The final consonant (group) of the stem is *palatal* for all persons in the imperfect indicative. And that is all you need to know about the imperfect indicative. That was not too bad, now was it?

VII.b.3. Imperative
(*GOI*: §§583-95; Lehmann: 21-2, 55, 101; McCone: 80-1, 103-5, 112-3; Quin: lesson 18; Stifter: 180-5; Strachan: 38-9, 42-3; Tigges: 46, 108)

The imperative is used if you want to give someone an order, e.g. go to the store! Let him get me some coffee! Stay away from the cookies! In English, you really only use the imperative with two persons: the second person singular (go! look! etc.) and the second person plural (go (ye)! look (ye)! etc.). In Old Irish, there are special forms for all the persons (perhaps with the exception of the first person singular. We don't really have any forms for that person. Besides, you usually don't go around giving yourself orders, unless you are Hamlet). For the other persons, you can make use of the verb 'let', or 'must':

Sg. 1.   (let me/I must go to the store!)
Sg. 2.   go to the store!
Sg. 3.   let him (her, it)/he (she, it) must go to the store!
Pl. 1.   let us/we must go to the store!
Pl. 2.   go (ye) to the store!
Pl. 3.   let them/they must go to the store!

The imperative is formed with the present stem, as you know, so any endings for it you have to add to the present stem, e.g. *ben-*, *marb-*, *beir-*. Now, what exactly do those endings look like?

With the exception of the second and third person singular, the endings look the same as the **conjunct endings of the present indicative**. The second person singular has **no ending** and the third person singular ends in **–ed** or **–ad**.

You will be glad to know that there is only one form – so the same form is used for both independent (absolute/deuterotonic) and dependent (conjunct/prototonic) verbal forms.

Let me put it in an overview for you, to make it clearer. I am leaving out the first person singular, because it has not been very well attested (that means that so far, we haven't really found any texts in which we find this particular verbal form).

I am giving you examples from all the different kinds of verb that we have seen (strong verbs from the *beirid*-group (Thurneysen calls these BI verbs) – here the examples are from *teichid* 'flees' – I could have just used *beirid*, but that would have been boring; from the *gaibid*-group (BII verbs) – here the verb used is *guidid* 'prays'; from the *benaid*-group (BIV verbs) – I chose *crenaid* 'buys'; weak verbs from the *marbaid*-group (AI verbs), here *glanaid* 'cleans' and the *léicid*-group (AII verbs), here *dáilid* 'distributes'):

		teichid	*guidid*	*crenaid*	*glanaid*	*dáilid*
		'flees'	'prays'	'buys'	'cleans'	'distributes'
Sg.	2.	*teich*	*guid*	*cren*	*glan*	*dáil*
Sg.	3.	*teiched*	*guided*	*crenad*	*glanad*	*dáiled*
Pl.	1.	*techam*	*guidem*	*crenam*	*glanam*	*dáilem*

Pl.	2.	*teichid*	*guidid*	*crenaid*	*glanaid*	*dáilid*
Pl.	3.	*techat*	*guidet*	*crenat*	*glanat*	*dáilet*

Note that the verbs from the *beirid*-group (the BI verbs) have a fluctuating root in the imperative, exactly following the pattern of the present indicative (with the final consonant (group) of the stem neutral in the first person singular, first person plural and third person plural, and palatal in the second person singular, third person singular and second person plural).

Compound verbs in the imperative look like they are standing in their prototonic form, i.e. *tabair!* 'bring!' instead of **do-beir!* This is the usual form. But note that if you need to use an **infixed pronoun**, if you want to say something like 'let him bring me to the island', you use the deuterotonic form with the above endings. The translation for this sentence into Old Irish would be *dom-beired cosin n-insi*. If you need to use an infixed pronoun with a simple verb like marbaid, and there are no other particles there, you use the particle *no*, e.g. *na-marbat* 'let them kill him'. In these cases, it may be tricky to figure out whether you are dealing with a regular present indicative or with an imperative. So beware!

If you want to put the imperative in the **negative** (so if you want to say 'do *not* go to the concert!' etc.), you use the particle *ná*: *ná cren!* 'do not buy', *ná glanat* 'let them not clean'. You use the forms I have given you above after *ná*. Like I said: there is only one set of endings. Cool huh?

Note: There are actually four different negative particles in Old Irish, *ní* (your regular negative), *ná* (with the imperative), *nád* (in relative clauses) and *innád* (in questions, like 'does he not...?'). They are discussed below, in section VII.g.1 (the negative of the interrogative particle also in VII.g.2).

VII.c. Subjunctive stem
(*GOI*: §§596-632; Lehmann: 29-30; McCone: 121-34; Quin: lessons 19, 20-1, 24; Stifter: 265-78; Strachan: 43-51; Tigges: 76-80, 87-9)

We have already looked at some different tenses, but now, we are going to deal with a different **mood**. We have so far mostly looked at the indicative mood. Remember the terms present indicative and imperfect indicative? Well, the first word indicates what **tense** you have to deal with – present, imperfect, future, secondary future, preterite or perfect are the options – and the second word indicates the **mood** – indicative, imperative (yup, I snuck that one by you without mentioning it is actually a different mood) or subjunctive.

The **indicative** is your regular no-nonsense mood. The **imperative**, as you know, expresses an order. The **subjunctive** can be used for a number of different things. The most common one is probably to express a wish. In English you use the verb 'may', e.g. 'may he live long'. In Modern Irish you still find a subjunctive in sentences like *go raibh maith agat* 'thank you'. It is often found after conjunctions or particles expressing incertainty, like 'although' (*cé*) and 'if' (*ma, día*).

Another thing for which the subjunctive, especially the past subjunctive in connection with a secondary future, is often used, is to express an impossibility, as in 'if I could, I would go to the movies with you (implying 'but I can't).' The best strategy when you encounter a subjunctive (apart perhaps from getting yourself a stiff drink) is to translate it with 'may' first and take it from there. Eventually, you will get used to it. Don't worry!

Now, apart from the different tenses that the subjunctive has, the **present** subjunctive and the **past** subjunctive, there are two main kinds of subjunctive in Old Irish: the *ā*-subjunctive and the *s*-subjunctive. So when do you find an *ā*-subjunctive and when do you find an *s*-subjunctive?

You find an *s*-subjunctive only with **strong verbs** of which the root/stem ends in a **guttural or velar** (so the letters *c/g/ch*), a **dental** (so *t/th* or *d/lenited d*) or **−nn**.

You get an *ā*-subjunctive in **all other cases**, so for all **weak verbs** and for all **strong verbs** of which the root/stem **does NOT end** in a guttural, dental or *−nn*.

Note: Some grammars also discuss an *e*-subjunctive, see Stifter: 270 and McCone: 125-6. This type of subjunctive is only found with hiatus verbs of the second group (that is, with a stem ending in *−i*). The final *−i* found in the present stem is replaced by an *−e* which becomes a long *e* (*é*) if it is the final letter of the form. The endings are (with the exception of 1 sg.) the same as the endings of the *ā*-subjunctive, and in fact, in compound verbs when the stem is unstressed (e.g. *ní dé**nai*** where the actual verbal stem is unstressed) the endings of the *ā*-subjunctive are used. But not all grammars discuss the *e*-subjunctive – Thurneysen treats these verbs under the *ā*-subjunctive, for example (*GOI* §608). Because of this reason, and the fact it is so rare, I will not discuss it further here.

VII.c.1. The *ā*-subjunctive[34]

(*GOI*:§§597-612; Lehmann: 29-30; McCone: 122-5, 133-4; Quin: lesson 19-21; Stifter: 265-69, 274-5, 277; Strachan: 43-9; Tigges: 77-8, 88)

With the *ā*-subjunctive, the ending of the verbal stem is neutral for all the verbs except the ones in the *léicid*-group. This means that the BI-verbs (the *beirid*-group) that have an *ā*-subjunctive will have a stem ending in a neutral final consonant group for all the persons. It also means that all the verbs that belong to the BII or *gaibid*-group that have an *ā*-subjunctive now end in a neutral consonant.

Present *ā*-subjunctive

The subjunctive stem itself does not look that different from the present stem, with one big exception: the verbs from the *benaid*-group (BIV). Remember I told you that they end in a neutral –*n* in the present stem? Well, they only have that –*n* in the present stem. In all other stems they drop it. That means that the subjunctive stem for *crenaid* becomes *cre*- or *crí*-, and the endings are tacked on to that. Be mindful of this when translating – if you do not remember this, you may waste hours searching in vain in *DIL*. Now, let us look at the pattern for the endings in the present *ā*-subjunctive:

		Absolute	**Conjunct**
Sg.	1.	-(*e*)*a*	- none
	2.	-(*a*)*e*	-(*a*)*e*
	3.	-(*a*)*id*	-(*e*)*a*
Pl.	1.	-*m*(*a*)*i*	-*am*/*em*
	2.	-*th*(*a*)*e*	-(*a*)*id*
	3.	-(*a*)*it*	-*at*/*et*

As you can see, there are only a few endings that look different from the endings we have seen so far, all in the singular (highlighted above). In order to help you, let me give you some examples of the present *ā*-subjunctive:

		beirid		*marbaid*		*léicid*	
		Abs.	**Conj.**	**Abs.**	**Conj.**	**Abs.**	**Conj.**
Sg.	1.	*bera*	-*ber*	*marba*	-*marb*	*léicea*	-*léic*
	2.	*berae*	-*berae*	*marbae*	-*marbae*	*léice*	-*léice*
	3.	*beraid*	-*bera*	*marbaid*	-*marba*	*léicid*	-*léicea*

---

[34] Note that in the sections on subjunctive, future and preterite, the chapters are primarily sub-divided by types of subjunctive, future and preterite, rather than the different tenses (i.e. present subjunctive and past subjunctive etc.).

	beirid		*marbaid*		*léicid*	
	Abs.	**Conj.**	**Abs.**	**Conj.**	**Abs.**	**Conj.**
Pl.	1. *bermai*	*-beram*	*marbmai*	*-marbam*	*léicmi*	*-léicem*
	2. *berthae*	*-beraid*	*marbthae*	*-marbaid*	*léicthe*	*-léicid*
	3. *berait*	*-berat*	*marbait*	*-marbat*	*léicit*	*-léicet*

That is not too difficult, now is it? Just make sure that you look especially carefully in a text to see whether you are dealing with a verb form in the indicative or in the subjunctive, since a lot of the forms look the same!

Past *ā*-subjunctive

Time for some good news. The past *ā*-subjunctive is very easy. As you know, if you have read the section on the imperfect indicative, all you need to do is add the set of secondary endings that you learned there. In case you have forgotten them, these are the secondary endings:

		Active	**Passive**
Sg.	1.	*-(a)inn*	---
	2.	*-th(e)a*	---
	3.	*-ed / -ad*	*-th(a)e*
Pl.	1.	*-mais*	---
	2.	*-th(a)e*	---
	3.	*-t(a)is*	*-t(a)is*

Isn't that nice: you don't even have to learn different endings, because you know them already!

This does mean, however, that the only time where you can see a difference in form between a verb in the imperfect indicative and in the past subjunctive is if the subjunctive stem ends in a neutral consonant, whereas the indicative ends in a palatal vowel. If both stems end in a neutral vowel, you will NOT see a difference. That can be tricky when you are translating. But enough about that. Let us look at some examples:

		Imperfect Indicative	*vs.*	**Past Subjunctive**
Sg.	1.	*no gaibinn, no marbainn*		*no gabainn, no marbainn*
	2.	*no gaibthea, no marbtha*		*no gabtha, no marbtha*
	3.	*no gaibed, no marbad*		*no gabad, no marbad*
Pl.	1.	*no gaibmis, no marbmais*		*no gabmais, no marbtais*
	2.	*no gaibthe, no marbthae*		*no gabthae, no marbthae*
	3.	*no gaibtis, no marbtais*		*no gabtais, no marbtais*

You can clearly see the difference between the imperfect indicative and the past subjunctive when looking at the verb *gaibid*, because that has a stem ending in a palatal consonant in the indicative stem, and a stem ending in a neutral consonant in the subjunctive stem; but you can see no difference at all between the imperfect indicative and the past subjunctive in the verb *marbaid* – because in both cases, the stem ends in a neutral consonant!

VII.c.2. The *s*-subjunctive

(*GOI*: §§613-32; Lehmann: -; McCone: 127-31, 133-4; Quin: lesson 22, 24; Stifter: 271-5, 277-8; Strachan: 49-51; Tigges: 78-9, 88)

Present *s*-subjunctive

Now that you (hopefully) have mastered the principles of the *ā*-subjunctive, we can go on to the other type of subjunctive stem that is found in Old Irish: the *s*-subjunctive. The *s*-subjunctive, you will remember, is only found with strong verbs ending in a dental (that is, -*d*, *t*, or –*th*), guttural or velar (-*g*, -*c*, or –*ch*) or –*nn*. As the term *s*-subjunctive suggests, these verbal endings are characterized by the letter '*s*'.

In most of the verbs belonging to this group, you will find the letter *s* in all forms **except the third person singular conjunct**. I said 'in most', because some of the verbs belonging to this group undergo a change, as a result of which you *never* find the letter *s*. All of these verbs that undergo that change have a stem in which the final consonant is preceded by –*r* or –*l*. We shall take a look at some of these later on. Now, let's first take a look at the pattern of the present *s*-subjunctive:

Active

		Absolute	Conjunct	Quality of *s*
Sg.	1.	-*su*	-*s*	neutral
	2.	-*si*	-*is*	palatal
	3.	-*is*	no ending, no –*s*	palatal
Pl.	1.	-*smai*	-*sam*	neutral
	2.	-*ste*	-*sid*	palatal
	3.	-*s(a)it*	-*sat*	neutral

Note that the pattern regarding the quality (neutral or palatal) of the *s* basically follows that of the *beirid*-group in the present indicative, that is to say, a pattern in which the first persons singular and plural and third person plural have a neutral ending, and the second persons singular and plural and the third person singular have a stem ending in a palatal consonant (singular: neutral – palatal – palatal, plural: neutral – palatal – neutral, remember?).

Here are the passive forms:

Passive

		Absolute	Conjunct
Sg.	3.	*-sair*	*-sar*
Pl.	3.	*-s(a)tair*	*-s(a)tar*

So what happens in the verbs that take an *s*-subjunctive but that have a stem of which the consonant before the final consonant ends in *–l* or *–r*, like *orcaid* 'slays'? These stems drop the final consonant, and, instead of adding an *s*, double the *l* or *r*.

Also, it is important to note that in the subjunctive stem a vowel change can occur; that is, the vowel you are familiar with from the present stem is replaced by another one. The verb *guidid*, 'prays', for example, has a subjunctive stem *gess-*. You will learn these things as you go along translating texts. Don't worry too much about them for the moment.

Let me give you some examples, so you can see what it would look like in a text. The verbs used are *téit*, 'goes', and *orcaid*, 'slays'. Note that the forms of *téit* have the diphthong *ía* in the forms that end in a neutral *s*, and *é* (+ *i*-glide) in the forms that end in palatal *s*.

Active

		Absolute	Conjunct
Sg.	1.	*tíasu, orru*	*-tías, -orr*
	2.	*tési, orri*	*-téis, -oirr*
	3.	*téis, oirr*	*-té, -or*
Pl.	1.	*tíasmai, orrmai*	*-tíasam, -oram*
	2.	*téiste, orrte*	*-téssid, -oirrid*
	3.	*tíasait, orrait*	*-tíasat, -orrat*

Passive

		Absolute	Conjunct
Sg.	3.	*tíasair, orrair*	*-tíasar, -orrar*
Pl.	3.	*tíastair, orrtair*	*-tíastar, -orrtar*

Deponent verbs

We do not really have many absolute forms of deponent verbs in the *s*-subjunctive (see *GOI* §621). The forms that we do have all belong to the *midithir* group (there are no weak verbs with an *s*-subjunctive, remember!). The only examples that we have from texts are *meser*, 'you may judge', the 2

118

sg. abs. *s*-subjunctive of *midithir*, and a third person singular *estir*, and 3 sg. relative *mestar*. Note the delenition of the *–th* after the letter *s*!

		Absolute	Conjunct
Sg.	1.	not attested; perhaps *-sur*	-sur
	2.	-ser	-ser
	3.	-stir	-star
Pl.	1.	not attested; perhaps *-saimmir*	-sammar
	2.	not attested; perhaps *-ste*	-sid
	3.	not attested; perhaps *-saitir*	-satar

The passive endings for the deponent verbs are the same as for the active verbs – so I do not have to discuss them here. Just add the appropriate endings above and voilà!

Past *s*-subjunctive

Again, the past subjunctive is very easy. You simply take the subjunctive stem and add the endings we have seen before, the same endings that we used with the *ā*-subjunctive and the imperfect indicative (you should know these by now) to the form with the *s*:

		Active	Passive
Sg.	1.	-(a)inn	---
	2.	-th(e)a	---
	3.	-ed / -ad	-th(a)e
Pl.	1.	-mais	---
	2.	-th(a)e	---
	3.	-t(a)is	-t(a)is

Is that easy, or what? An example, to illustrate it (I am using the verbs *guidid*, 'prays' and *orcaid*, 'slays', with subjunctive stems *gess-* and *orr-* respectively):

Sg.	1.	no gessainn, no orrain
	2.	no gesta, no orrta
	3.	no gessed, no oirred
Pl.	1.	no gesmais, no orrmais
	2.	no gestae, no orrtae
	3.	no gestais, no orrtais

Passive:

Sg. 3.   *no gestae, no orrtae*
Pl.   3.   *no gestais, no orrtais*

And this brings us to the…(*insert drum roll here*)

VII.d. Future stem
(*GOI*: §§633-69; Lehmann: 44-5, 78, 118; McCone: 135-50; Quin: lessons 27-9, 31; Stifter: 282-94; Strachan: 52-60; Tigges: 94-8, 100-1)

Here we are at a new milestone: the third verbal stem! See, you are basically a pro now. Like the indicative, the future is a **tense** (as opposed to the subjunctive, which is a **mood**). The most common kinds of future are: the *f*-future, the reduplicated and *ē*-future, and the *s*-future.[35] The *f*-future is used by almost all weak verbs and by some strong verbs; the reduplicated and *ē*-future is used by most strong verbs that take the *ā*-subjunctive and the *s*-future is used by most strong verbs that take the *s*-subjunctive (i.e. with a stem ending in guttural, dental or *–nn*). Finally, there are a few suppletive futures – this means that some verbs use a completely different verb to supply the verbal forms of the future tense. I will refer to those very briefly at the end of this section.

VII.d.1. The *f*-future
(*GOI*: §§635-44; Lehmann: 44-5, 78, 118; McCone: 135-8, 147-8; Quin: lessons 27-8; Stifter: 282-84, 293-4; Strachan: 52-5; Tigges: 94-6, 101)

The *f*-future is, as I have just mentioned, used by almost all weak verbs (the verb *caraid* 'loves' is one of the exceptions) and by some strong verbs, namely compounds of *–icc* (like *ro-icc* 'reaches', *do-icc* 'comes' and *con-icc* 'is able'), compounds of *–muinethar*, and sometimes compounds of *–em* (see *GOI* §634).

As the name suggests, you will find the letter *f-* in (almost) all of the verbal forms. The stem of the *f*-future basically looks like the present stem with *–f(a)-* added to it. To the future stem, you then add the endings of the *ā*-

---

[35] There is also an *i*-future, found in hiatus verbs and verbs from the *benaid*-group that have a future stem ending in a vowel (remember that the *n* found in the *benaid*-group is only present in the present stem), but it is very rare, so I omit it here. See McCone: 141-2 and Stifter: 286-7. McCone and Stifter also combine the reduplicated future formed on the *ā*-subjunctive and the *ē*-future and refer to that as the *a*-future.

subjunctive. Isn't that great? You already know the endings!

There is one exception: the first person singular conjunct active. This form has no -f- and ends in -ub, with a lenited b. Let us take a look at the pattern, and compare it with the ā-subjunctive, so you can see that you are dealing with largely the same endings:

Active

		f-future		ā-subjunctive	
		Absolute	**Conjunct**	**Absolute**	**Conjunct**
Sg.	1.	-f-(e)a	**-ub**	-(e)a	**no ending**
	2.	-f-(a)e	-f-a, -f-e	-(a)e	-(a)e
	3.	-f-(a)id	-f-(e)a	-(a)id	-(e)a
Pl.	1.	-f-(a)immi	-f-am, -f-em	-m(a)i	-am/em
	2.	-f-(a)ithe/ -fa(i)de	-f-(a)id	-th(a)e	-(a)id
	3.	-f-(a)it	-f-at, -f-et	-(a)it	-at/et

The differences you can see can be found in the first person singular conjunct. Although the 1 and 2 pl. look a little different, they aren't really: you sometimes find an extra vowel in verbal forms and other words because they would be impossible to pronounce otherwise, e.g. the verbal form *léic-f-de, which becomes léicfide.

Passive

		f-future		ā-subjunctive	
		Absolute	**Conjunct**	**Absolute**	**Conjunct**
Sg.	3.	-f(a)-idir	-f(a)-ider	-thair	-thar
Pl.	3.	-f(a)-itir	-f(a)-iter	-tair	-tar

Note: I don't know if you have noticed it in texts that you are translating, but a lot of the time, verbs with an *f*-future have palatal endings, where you would expect neutral endings (for example with the verb *marbaid*). It has been explained to me that the *–f* here has a strong tendency to make things palatal, but that later pressure from speakers changed those palatal endings to neutral ones.

Deponent verbs
There are not many examples of deponent verbs in the *f*-future found in texts, but the paradigm for the endings is the following:

		Absolute	Conjunct
Sg.	1.	*-f-ar/ -f-er*	*-f-ar/ -f-er*
	2.	*-f-(a)ider*	*-f-(a)ider*
	3.	*-f-(a)ithir/ f-(a)idir*	*-f-adar/ -f-edar*
Pl.	1.	*-f-(a)immir*	*-f-ammar/ -f-emmar*
	2.	*-f-(a)ide*	*-f-(a)id*
	3.	*-f-(a)itir*	*-f-atar/ -f-etar*

The passive forms are (as you might expect) the same as above.

The conditional of the *f*-future

The conditional (also called the secondary future) of the *f*-future is formed by adding the secondary endings to the future stem — yes, those same endings we have seen for the imperfect indicative and past subjunctive that of course you know by heart at this stage. For the last time, here are those secondary endings:

		Active	Passive
Sg.	1.	*-(a)inn*	---
	2.	*-th(e)a*	---
	3.	*-ed / -ad*	*-th(a)e*
Pl.	1.	*-mais*	---
	2.	*-th(a)e*	---
	3.	*-t(a)is*	*-t(a)is*

An example (note that the root ending is often palatal because of that tendency of the *f* to make things palatal):

Sg.	1.	*no mairbf-inn*
	2.	*no mairbf-e-da* (with helping vowel; *you* try pronouncing **marbftha* without help)
	3.	*no mairbf-ed, no marbf-ad*
Pl.	1.	*no mairbf-i-(m)mis*
	2.	*no mairbf-i-the, no léicf-i-de*
	3.	*no mairbf-i-tis, no marbf-ai-tis*

Passive

Sg.	*no mairbf-i-de*
Pl.	*no mairbf-i-tis*

VII.d.2. Reduplicated and other futures and conditionals

In this section, I will first discuss the regular reduplicated future, based on the *ā*-subjunctive; then, I will talk about *ē*-future, because that also follows the pattern of the *ā*-subjunctive. After that, I will take a look at the reduplicated *s*-future, and finally I will say something very briefly about suppletive verbs.

The 'normal' reduplicated future, formed on the *ā*-subjunctive

(*GOI*: §645 ff.; Lehmann: - ; McCone: 138-42; Quin: lesson 29; Stifter: 288-9; Strachan: 55-8; Tigges: 96-7, 101)

You can basically find this future **with strong verbs that have an *ā*-subjunctive** (please note that weak verbs almost always have an *f*-future). The process is really very simple:

Step 1. Take the stem of the *ā*-subjunctive
Example: *canaid*, subjunctive stem *can*-.

Step 2. Double (reduplicate) the first consonant of the stem
For the stem *can*-, this is the letter *c*-. This gives you *ccan-.

Step 3. Add a reduplication vowel
Originally, this vowel was the letter *i* (cp. *GOI* §646), but you very often find the letter *e* as the reduplication vowel if the syllable before which it stands is a neutral syllable (i.e. does not contain the letters *i* or *e*). For *can*-, in which *c*- is a neutral consonant, we do in fact find this *e*. The form we now have is *c-e-can.

Step 4. Lenite the first letter of the original stem
You find lenition because the consonant that marks the beginning of the *ā*-subjunctive stem now stands between two vowels, and as we have seen way back in the beginning, a consonant that stands between two vowels is lenited. The form with *can*- that we find is therefore *cechan*-.

Step 5. You now add the desired endings of the *ā*-subjunctive
If you want a form in the secondary future, just add the secondary endings we have seen above. Look out for syncope when you add the endings! Also, in the plural, you might find an extra vowel there, to help in pronunciation.

Here is the pattern for *canaid* 'sings'. I am comparing it with the *ā*-subjunctive, so you can see that the endings really are the same:

Active

		Present *ā*-subjunctive		Reduplicated future	
		Absolute	**Conjunct**	**Absolute**	**Conjunct**
Sg.	1.	*cana*	*-can*	*cechna*[36]	*-cechan*
	2.	*canae*	*-canae*	*cechnae*	*-cechnae*
	3.	*canaid*	*-cana*	*cechnaid*	*-cechna*
Pl.	1.	*canmai*	*-canam*	**cechnaimmi*	*-cechnam*
	2.	*cantae*	*-canaid*	**cechnaithe*	*-cechnaid*
	3.	*canait*	*-canat*	*cechnait*	*-cechnat*

The first and second persons plural active have not been found in any manuscript yet, so we will have to reconstruct them for the moment - which is what the asterisk stands for. In the passive, I am using the verb *beirid* for the *ā*-subjunctive forms, in order to better show you the different endings (the reason for this is that the 3 sg. *-thair* ending for *canaid* would be delenited because of the letter *n*):

Passive

		Present *ā*-subjunctive		Reduplicated future	
		Absolute	**Conjunct**	**Absolute**	**Conjunct**
Sg.	3.	*ber**thair***	*-ber**thar***	*cechn**aithir***	*-cechn**athar***
Pl.	3.	*ber**tair***	*-ber**tar***	*cechn**aitir***	*-cechn**atar***

Can you see that (apart from the added vowel for pronunciation) the endings are the same? Now, the conditional or secondary future. Again, I shall compare it with the pattern for the past subjunctive. Forms that have not been attested are indicated with an asterisk:

Active

		Past *ā*-subjunctive	Secondary future
Sg.	1.	*no canainn*	*no cechnainn*
	2.	*no canta*	**no cechnatha*
	3.	*no canad*	*no cechnad*
Pl.	1.	*no canmais*	**no cechnaimmis*
	2.	*no cantae*	**no cechnaithe*
	3.	*no cantais*	**no cechnaitis*

---

[36] Note the syncope: *can-a* becomes **cechan-a*, then the vowel of the second syllable (*a*) is syncopated. Since this is a neutral vowel, the consonant group remains neutral. See if you can figure out the syncope patterns for the other persons – that should be a breeze!

Passive

		Past *ā*-subjunctive	Secondary future
Sg.	3.	*no cantae*	**no cechnaithe*
Pl.	3.	*no cantais*	**no cechnaitis*

See, that is not so bad, is it? Now, on to the next type of future, the *ē*-future ('long e-future').

The *ē*-future

(*GOI*: §650 ff; Lehmann: - ; McCone: 139-40; Quin: - ; Stifter: 289; Strachan: 58; Tigges: 96-7, 101)

The *ē*-future may be found with a number of **strong verbs**:
   (1) that take the *ā*-subjunctive
   (2) that have either *e*- or *a*- in the subjunctive stem
   (3) that do not have a reduplicated future

Some of the most commonly used verbs have an *ē*-future, like *beirid* 'carries' (and therefore also the compounds of *beirid*, like *do-beir* 'brings, gives'), *gaibid* 'gets, seizes' and *do-gní* 'does'.

The process for the *ē*-future is even simpler than the reduplicated future. Are you ready?

Step 1. You take the *ā*-subjunctive stem
Examples: *gaibid*, subjunctive stem *gab-* and *beirid*, subjunctive stem *ber-*

Step 2. You change the vowel of the *ā*-subjunctive stem to -*é*-
This gives you *géb-* and *bér-*.

Step 3. You add the desired ending of the present or past *ā*-subjunctive in order to get the right person in the ē-future or ē-conditional, for example *no gébainn*, 'I would seize', *bérmai* 'we will carry', etc.

And that is it! Now, let's move on to the reduplicated *s*-future.

The reduplicated *s*-future

(*GOI*: §657ff.; Lehmann:; McCone: 142-4; Quin: lesson 29; Stifter: 285-6; Strachan: 59-60; Tigges: 97-8, 101)[37]

This one is also very simple - you should have no trouble with it. The *s*-future is found with verbs that take the *s*-subjunctive. Just to freshen up your memory: the *s*-subjunctive is used with strong verbs with a present stem that ends in a velar or guttural (*c, ch* or *g*), a dental (*d, th* or *t*) or *-nn*. An example of this is the verb *guidid* 'prays, beseeches'.

Now, the reduplication process is exactly the same as the one described above: you take the subjunctive stem, in the case of *guidid* that is *ges-*; you then double the first consonant of the subjunctive stem, that is the letter *g-*. You add the reduplication vowel; since *ges(s)* is a palatal syllable, this is the letter *i*; and then you lenite the first letter of the subjunctive stem (but of course, lenition of the letter *g* is not shown in Old Irish). The outcome then is...wait for it...: *gigis*.

Then, as may be expected from the name, you add the endings of the *s*-subjunctive to the future stem, and this is what you get, bearing in mind the potential for syncope:

Active

		s-subjunctive		*s*-future	
		Absolute	**Conjunct**	**Absolute**	**Conjunct**
Sg.	1.	*gessu*	*-gess*	*gigsu*	*-gigius*
	2.	*gessi*	*-geiss*	*gigsi*	*-gigis*
	3.	*geiss*	*-gé*	*gigis*	**-gig*
Pl.	1.	*gesmai*	*-gessam*	*gigsimmi*	*-gigsem*
	2.	*geiste*	*-geissid*	*gigeste*	*-gigsid*
	3.	*gessait*	*-gessat*	*gigsit*	*-gigset*

The only different forms are found in the 3 sg. passive absolute and conjunct, where the *-th-* makes its triumphant return:

Passive

		s-subjunctive		*s*-future	
		Absolute	**Conjunct**	**Absolute**	**Conjunct**
Sg.	3.	*gessair*	*-gessar*	**gigsithir*	**-gigsethar*
Pl.	3.	*gessitir*	*-gessatar*	*gigsitir*	*-gigsetar*

---

[37] There is also an unreduplicated form of the *s*-future. This is found with some of the strong verbs that have an *s*-subjunctive, but it is so rare that I will not discuss it here – for further information see Stifter: 284, McCone: 142.

Suppletive verbs in the future

As stated above, there are some verbs that use a completely different verbal stem in the future (this occurs for the preterite as well). One of the most common verbs, *téit* 'goes' is one of them. The future stem of *téit* is *riga-/rega-*. Remember this form, or you will spend an awfully long time looking up this form in *DIL* later. Or at the very least remember that the paradigms of a number of the most common and irregular verbs, including *téit*, can for example be found in Strachan's *Paradigms* (p. 74 ff.), in *GOI* §757 ff. and in Antony Green's handy little book *Old Irish verbs and vocabulary*. That might save you some time.

See, this section was not so bad! Now, get yourself some tea or coffee and possibly a cookie (I am partial to chocolate chip myself) - you have earned it.

VII.e. The preterite and perfect active and deponent

(*GOI*: §§670-704; Lehmann: 37-8, 112; McCone: 85-91, 114-15; Quin: lessons 34-8; Stifter: 199-205, 213-20; Strachan: 61-7; Tigges: 62, 118-22, 150, 152-9)

In this section, we finally meet the fourth verbal stem, the **preterite active**. The preterite stem is used to make two past tenses, that of the **preterite**, and that of the **perfect**. The other past tense we have seen so far is the imperfect indicative, formed by adding different endings to the present stem. To freshen up your memory, the imperfect indicative is used to indicate a continuous or repetitive action in the past that has not yet been completed, often translated with the addition of 'used to', e.g. 'he used to walk to school every day'. But not all action in the past is continuous or repetitive, so we need another past tense. And this is where the preterite and perfect come in.

The preterite is most commonly used in stories, so it is also often called a narrative past tense. The preterite expresses a single action: 'he went to the doctor's', 'he won the lottery'. The perfect is used to express an action that has been completed at the time of speaking, or a result of an action (from Latin *perfectum*, 'done entirely, through and through'). The perfect is usually translated into English by using 'to have': 'he has died', 'he has seen that movie'. In a handy overview, this is what we get:

Imperfect indicative: indicates continuous or repetitive action in the past (that has not yet been completed); translated often by adding 'used to' – 'he used to go'.

| Preterite: | expresses a single action in the past ('he went'), and is also often used in stories as a narrative past tense. |
| **Perfect**: | expresses an action that has been completed at the time of speaking ('he has gone'), or the result of an action ('he has died' = 'he is dead'). The perfect is usually translated by adding the auxiliary verb ('helping verb') 'to have'. |

Now the preterite, as the subjunctive and future, comes in different kinds. The most common ones are the *s*-preterite and the *t*-preterite, and we also have a number of what we call suffixless preterites (this includes the reduplicated preterite,[38] preterite formations marked by a long vowel, as well as the suppletive verbs). The term 'suffixless' merely refers to the fact that these kinds of preterite do not have an extra letter added to the stem (the *s*-preterite has an added *s*; the *t*-preterite has (surprise) an added *t*).

VII.e.1. The *s*-preterite
(*GOI*: §§672-81; Lehmann: 37-8, 112; McCone: 85-6, 114-15; Quin: lessons 34-5; Stifter: 199-202, 204-5; Strachan: 61-2; Tigges: 62, 118-19)

The *s*-preterite is the one that you'll find most often. It is used with almost all weak verbs, and with a number of strong verbs. It is basically formed by adding the letter –*s* to the verbal root, followed by an ending. The endings look a lot like those found with the *s*-subjunctive, and with the present indicative of the BI (or '*beirid*') group. The only form that does not contain the letter *s* (and of course the form found most often) is the **third person singular conjunct**. Let's jump right in, shall we?

Active

	Absolute	Pattern	Conjunct	Pattern
Sg.	1. *marbsu* 'I killed'	ends in -*u*	-*marbus*	ends in -(*i*)*us*
	2. *marbsai* 'you killed'	ends in -*ai*	-*marbais*	ends in palatal *s*
	3. *marbais* 'he killed'	ends in palatal -*s*	-*marb*	no ending, no *s*
Pl.	1. *marbsaimmi* 'we killed'	ends in –(*aim*)*mi*	-*marbsam*	ends in neutral *m*

---

[38] It seems that a lot of the hiatus verbs have a combination of a reduplicated preterite and an *s*-preterite – see McCone: 91 and Stifter: 202. Since they are rare, I do not discuss them here.

2. *marbsaithe*   ends in -(*ai*)*the*   -*marbsaid*   ends in palatal *d*
'you killed'
3. *marbsait*   ends in palatal *t*   -*marbsat*   ends in neutral *t*
'they killed'

Deponent

For deponent verbs, we only really have found conjunct forms in the texts. This is the pattern for those forms:

		Conjunct	**Pattern**	**Meaning**
Sg.	1.	-*labrasur*	ends in —*ur*	'I spoke'
	2.	-*labraister*	ends in —*ther*, but delenition after *s*	'you spoke'
	3.	-*labrastar*	ends in —*thar*, but delenition after *s*	'he spoke'
Pl.	1.	-*labrasammar*	ends in —*ammar*/ -*emmar*	'we spoke'
	2.	-*labraisid*	ends in palatal *d*	'you spoke'
	3.	-*labrasatar*	ends in —*atar*/ -*etar*	'they spoke'

And that is the *s*-preterite. Now, the good news: if you want to turn a preterite into a perfect, all you need to do is add the particle *ro*, and put it before the **conjunct** form of the preterite. So *marbsu* is preterite, 'I killed', and you make it perfect by putting ro before the conjunct form, -*marbus*. This gives you *ro marbus* 'I have killed'. How's that? Not bad, eh?

Note: Nowadays, the form consisting of preterite + *ro* is often referred to as 'augmented preterite' rather than 'perfect'; I chose to use the term 'perfect' in this book, however, since that is the term found in most of the grammars, including *GOI*.

VII.e.2. The *t*-preterite
(*GOI*: §§682-85; Lehmann: 37-8, 112; McCone: 86-7, 114-5; Quin: lesson 36; Stifter: 202-5; Strachan: 63-4; Tigges: 62, 119-20)

The *t*-preterite is found with strong verbs of which the root ends in -*r*, -*l*, and some that end in -*m* and —*g* (if you need help remembering this, think of the word '**glam**our'). A *t*- is added to the root. When the root ends in —*r* or —*l*, the result is —*rt* and —*lt*; *-emt* results in —*ét*, and —*gt* gives us —*cht*.

It must be said that the absolute forms of the *t*-preterite are seldom found even in Old Irish. The pattern we can distinguish and predict looks a lot like the present indicative of the *beirid*-group of verbs, with an added *t*. Note the third person plural forms, however, ending in *–(ta)tar*! In case you haven't seen this before, forms with * before them mean they are not actually found in texts, but reconstructed:

		Absolute	**Pattern**	**Conjunct**	**Pattern**
Sg.	1.	**birtu*	ends in *–u*?	*-biurt*	*-u* is seen in verb
	2.	**birti*	ends in *–i*?	*-birt*	ends in palatal consonant (group)
	3.	*birt, oirt, milt*	ends in pal. cons. (group)	*-bert, -ort*	ends in neutral consonant (group)
Pl.	1.	??		*-bert(am)mar*	ends in *–(am)mar*
	2.	??		*-bertid*	ends in *–(a)id*
	3.	??		*-bertatar*	ends in *–(ta)tar*

As with the *s*-preterite, the perfect (or augmented preterite) is usually formed by putting *ro* before the conjunct forms, so *ro ort* 'he has killed'.

VII.e.3. The suffixless preterites

The reduplicated preterite
(*GOI*: §§687-91; Lehmann: 37-8; McCone: 88-91, 115; Quin: lesson 37; Stifter: 213-15, 220; Strachan: 64-6; Tigges: 62, 120-1)

Reduplication is found with a number of strong verbs. It is formed in pretty much the same way as the reduplicated future: by doubling the initial consonant, adding a vowel (usually *-e-*, sometimes *-o-*) and leniting the original consonant. An example of this is *canaid*, with stem *can-*, which becomes *cechan*. If a verb begins with *sl-* or *sn-*, this becomes *sel-* and *sen-* (this makes sense, of course, because of the lenited second *s*: **sesl-*, **sesn-*).

The forms mostly look the same in absolute and conjunct, and we don't have a 2 pl. absolute, but this is the general pattern:

		Example	**Pattern**
Sg.	1.	*cechan*	ends in neutral final consonant of the stem
	2.	*cechan*	ends in neutral final consonant of the stem
	3.	*cechain*	ends in palatal final consonant of the stem
Pl.	1.	*cechnammar*	ends in *–emmar, -ammar*
	2.	*–cechnaid*	ends in palatal *d*
	3.	*cechnatar*	ends in *–atar/ -etar*

Be on your guard, because in some forms, the reduplication is hard to find, e.g. in *gén-* (with compensatory lengthening) from **gegn-* from the stem **gní-*.

The perfect (or augmented preterite) is formed by putting *ro* before the conjunct form, so *ro cechan* 'I have sung' or 'you have sung'. However, *ro* is unstressed. This means that if you put a conjunct particle before *ro cechan*, so **ní ro cechan*, the stress shifts to the particle *ro*. This is very similar to what happens with deuterotonic and prototonic forms. The reduplicated consonant is lenited and then lost (Quin calls this 'dissimilation'), and the *–o* from *ro* and the reduplication vowel now make a diphthong: **ní rochechan* becomes *ní roíchan*. Another example: **ní romemaid* becomes *ní roímaid*.

Preterites with long vowels and without (visible) reduplication
(*GOI*: §§692-702; Lehmann: - ; McCone: 89; Quin: lesson 38; Stifter: 215-18; Strachan: 66-7; Tigges: 121)

The *ā*-preterite
In the preterite stem of a small number of verbs, the vowel of the root (usually short *a* or short *e*) is simply replaced by *ā*, for example:

> *teichid* 'flees', with stem *tech-* becomes *tách-*
> *rethid* 'runs', with stem *reth-* becomes *ráth-*
> *guidid* 'prays', becomes *gád-* and so on.

With regard to endings, the same pattern is used that you find with *canaid* above (so 1/2 sg. pret. of *teichid* 'flees' is *tách*, 3 sg. is *táich* etc.).

The *ī*-preterite
Similarly, in some verbs, we find an *ī* replacing the root vowel:
midithir 'judges', with stem *mid-* becomes *míd-*
fichid 'fights', with stem *fich-* becomes *fích-*
The element *féd* in the verb *in-fét/ad-fét* 'relates' becomes *in-fíd*, and so on.
The active verbs follow the pattern described above, but in the case of the deponent *midithir*, the endings are as follows:

		Pattern
Sg.	1. *–ar*	stem + neutral *r*
	2. *–ar*	stem + neutral *r*
	3. *–air*	stem + palatal *r*
Pl.	1. *–ammar*	stem + *-ammar*
	2. *–id*	stem + *-id*
	3. *–atar*	stem + *-atar*

Suppletive verbs

(*GOI*: §§534,757-73, 694; Lehmann: - ; McCone: 89-90; Quin: lesson 38; Stifter: 219; Strachan: see 74ff under paradigms for some exx.; Tigges: 122)

Some verbs make use of a different verb to form the preterite or perfect tense. That different verb is called a **suppletive verb** (it supplies the necessary forms – this is also found sometimes in the future). The verb *beirid*, for example, uses forms with the root *ucc* to express the perfect (but remember that it has a *t*-preterite!). The verb *do-beir* even uses two suppletive verbs in the perfect. *Do-rat* is used to express 'he has given'; *do-ucc* 'he has brought'. However, *as-beir* does not use a suppletive verb in the perfect (*as-rubart* 'he has said'). It is probably easiest to learn these forms as you go, but some of the most common forms that you should definitely remember are:[39]

(1) ***ad-cí,*** with preterite *co n-accae* and perfect *ad-condairc. Co n-accae* occurs very often in texts, especially to introduce a new element. In dependent position, *-accae* is used for both preterite and perfect, because *ad-condairc* does not have a prototonic form.

(2) ***téit,*** which uses the preterite *luid*, but the perfect *do-cuaid;* the verb *do-téit* does the same thing, and has preterite *do-luid* and perfect *do-dechuid.*[40]

(3) ***do-icc.*** This verb (and other compounds of *icc* as well, like *ro-icc*) has only one form for both preterite and perfect: *do-ánaic, -tánaic.* Very often, the form *tánaic* is used in places where you would expect a deuterotonic form (really, it is a contraction of the preverb and the vowel of the stem. This also occurs often in the present tense, where you can find *ticc* instead of *do-icc* and in other verbs as well; the term for this that I recommend using is **contracted form**, coined by Peter Schrijver,[41] or **contracted deuterotonic**).

---

[39] Look in *GOI* for a large number of suppletive verbs and the verbs with which they are used.

[40] This verb also uses a suppletive verb for the future (*rega-/raga-*) – see the section on suppletive verbs under the future stem.

[41] See his book *Studies in the history of Celtic pronouns and particles*, Maynooth Studies in Linguistics II, Maynooth 1997 p. 115 ff.

VII.f. The preterite passive
(*GOI*: §§705-13; Lehmann: - ; McCone: 107-9; Quin: lesson 39; Stifter: 235-8; Strachan: 61-7; Tigges: 124-6, 153-9)

This is the fifth and final verbal stem used in Old Irish. Hurrah! You are almost there. It is used just as you would expect, like all the other passive tenses we have seen: no big deal. You know what to do already!

These are the basic endings:

Singular		Plural	
Absolute	**Conjunct**	**Absolute**	**Conjunct**
-th(a)e	*-d or –th*	*-th(a)i*	*-th(e)a*

There are some rules to remember, however:

(1) With strong verbs containing the groups *-er-* or *-el-*, you will find them as *-re-* and *-le-* in the preterite/perfect passive, e.g. *beirid*, 'carries' stem *ber-* has preterite passive singular conjunct *–breth*, *ceilid*, 'hides' stem *cel-* becomes *–cleth*.

(2) Verbal roots ending in a nasal, so *n* or *m*, become *–ét* in the preterite passive, e.g. *canaid*, 'sings' stem *can-* becomes preterite passive singular conjunct *–cét*; *daimid*, 'admits' stem *dam-* becomes *–dét*.

(3) Verbal roots ending in a dental or *s* become (neutral) *–ss*: *ro-fitir* 'knows' has *-fess*, *guidid* 'prays' becomes *gess*, *midithir* 'judges' becomes *mess*.

(4) Verbal roots ending in a guttural (*g,c,ch*) become *–cht*, as in *dligid* 'is entitled to', stem *dlig-*, becomes *–dlecht*; *fichid*, 'fights' becomes *fecht*; *-icc* 'reaches' becomes *–icht*; *ar-icc* becomes *–airecht*.

VII.g. Miscellaneous information relating to the verb

VII.g.1. Negative particles
(*GOI*: §§860-75; Lehmann: 70; McCone: (67, 96); Quin: - ; Stifter: 135; Strachan: - ; Tigges: 108)

There are four common negative particles, all conjunct particles:

(1) the most common negative particle is *ní* 'not', used in regular sentences ;

(2) the negative particle used to negate an imperative (so to say 'don't go!', 'don't hit that dog!' etc.) is *ná*

(3) the negative particle used in relative sentences is *nád* (so for example 'the man who doesn't go to the dentist regularly', 'the woman who does not want to sing a song', 'the student who does not want to give up on learning Old Irish' (that last one is you, by the way))

(4) the negative particle used in questions, meaning 'does…not' is *innád* – see the next section.

Sometimes, an infixed pronoun is attached to the negative particle. In the case of *ní*, the infixed pronoun will be a class A infixed pronoun; something more sinister happens to both *ná* and *nád* – they get special forms (very simplistically speaking, you get the form *ná*+*ch*+infixed pronoun class C, but without the *d* – see above, section V.b.4).

VII.g.2. Interrogative particles
(*GOI*: §463-5; Lehmann: 51, 69-70; McCone: (67); Quin: lessons 3,5; Stifter: 57, 71, 135; Strachan: - ; Tigges: 109)

The particle *in*
In Irish, if one wishes to ask a question, this question is preceded by an **interrogative particle** (if you have a hard time remembering this term, just think of the interrogation or questioning of a suspect by the police). The normal interrogative particle in Old Irish is *in*, which nasalizes the following verbal form. It is also a **conjunct particle**, so the following verbal form will stand either in the conjunct form (in the case of a simple verb) or in the prototonic form (in the case of a compound verb):

In mbeir *int ech in fer cosa thech?* 'Does the horse carry the man to his house?'
In tabair *int ech in fer cosa thech? '*Does the horse bring the man to his house?'

Note: if the question is one of the type 'whether…or', as in 'is the dress yellow or blue?', *in* can be used before each member (so in the preceding question it would be used before 'yellow' and 'blue'); but often, the second alternative is introduced by *fa/ fá/ ba/ bá*, which lenites a following word if it can.

The particle *innád*
There is also a negative interrogative particle, that is used when you want to ask questions like '**does** he **not** come home when he is supposed to?', or '**did** you **not** listen to your lecturer when (s)he was explaining the complexities of Old Irish grammar to you?' This particle is *innád*, which nasalizes the following verbal form.

Note: in the case of a negative question to which an affirmative answer is expected (for those of you who have studied Latin, questions where you would expect *nonne*), the question can be introduced either by *innád*, or by the conjunct particle *cani/ceni/cini*.

VII.g.3. The augmenting particle *ro*
(*GOI*: §§526-37; Lehmann: 37, 71; McCone: 45, 151-9; Quin: lesson 40; Stifter: 250-6; Strachan: 60 ff., see under paradigms; Tigges: 106-7)

The particle *ro*, sometimes also called the **augment** is found very often in Old Irish texts. In a nutshell: originally, the particle *ro* was a preposition (comparable to *pro* 'before'). In some cases, it was used as a preverb, but later in the Old Irish and in the Middle Irish period it became a conjunct particle.

Meanings and usages of the particle *ro*
(*GOI*: §§530-1; Lehmann:71; McCone:151-2; Quin: lesson 40; Stifter: 250-1; Strachan: -; Tigges: 106-7)

Here are the two most common usages of *ro*:

a. Completion
The particle *ro* is often used to indicate **completion of an action**. It can be used with the preterite, past subjunctive and imperfect to add this sense of completion. With the imperfect, it indicates an action that has been **repeatedly completed in the past**.

It can also be used with the present indicative and subjunctive. In this case, it indicates an action that has been completed **at the time another action takes place**, e.g. 'I am settling into life here after having moved here'. If the subjunctive is used in a future sense, it has the meaning of a perfective future, e.g. 'By this time tomorrow, we shall have won the battle.'

b. Possibility or ability
The particle *ro* can also be used with different moods and tenses in order to indicate a possibility or ability, for example with the present indicative: *as-ro-bair* 'he can say', or with the future: *ní de-r-génat*, 'they will not be able to do'.

The position of *ro*
(*GOI*: §§527 ff.; Lehmann: 71; McCone: 153-5; Quin: - ; Stifter: 254-6; Strachan: - ; Tigges: 106-7)

The matter of the position of *ro* is very complicated, so I will try to make it as easy as I can for now. You can always delve deeper into the issue at your own leisure, if you're a glutton for punishment.

Thurneysen described two main positions of *ro* in *GOI* (§§527-9), and referred to them as 'fixed *ro*' and 'movable *ro*', but McCone and Stifter give a far more detailed description, and the following is based in large part on their discussions.[42]

Let's begin with the easy part. If you want to add *ro* to an absolute form of the simple verb, you place it right before the conjunct verbal form – you know this already. Let's say you want to construct the form 'I have allowed'. You first take the preterite form, *léicsiu*, 'I allowed', with conjunct form – *léicius*, and then add *ro* to the conjunct form, giving you *ro léicius*, 'I have allowed'.

As you also know, if you want to make this form dependent, i.e., by adding a conjunct particle to that, for example *ní*, *ro* moves to the stressed position, in exactly the same way that you have seen with the compound verbs – remember *beirid, -beir*, **do**-*beir, ní* **tabair**. If possible, **syncope** will take place, in this case giving you *ro léicius*, *ní reilcius, and, just as is the case for all preverbal particles ending in a vowel, it will **cause lenition** of the initial consonant of the verbal form if it can (so for example *ro cas* 'she bent', *ní rochas* 'she did not bend, or *ro car*, 'he has loved', *ní rochar*, 'he has not loved', this last example in McCone: 153).

So far, this is not too challenging, I hope. But of course it gets worse: the situation is much more complex in the case of compound verbs. Hold on to your horses – here we go!

Stage I.
Originally, in compound verbs, *ro* was almost always placed **directly before the verbal stem**, regardless of stress (McCone refers to this behavior of *ro* as '**preverbal**'),[43] and the rule was that it could NEVER stand at the beginning of the compound verb.[44] This corresponds to what Thurneysen

---

[42] See also McCone's *The early Irish verb*, p. 90 and p. 147ff.

[43] McCone: 153.

[44] The position of the augment *ro* really depended on the preverbal particle(s). As

called 'fixed *ro*' – compare the forms *do-ru-ménar* 'I have thought' and *nicon-tormb̄énar*, 'I have not thought', with *ro* immediately before the verb part – *ménar*. Once again, this position of *ro* **has absolutely nothing to do with stress** – in *do-ruménar*, the stress falls on *ru*; in *–tormb̄énar*, it falls on *to(r)*.

But this could of course cause an issue: since an extra syllable (*ro*) was added to the verbal form, this might cause syncope (like in the example – *tormb̄énar* above), and this, combined with other factors, meant that deuterotonic and prototonic verbal forms could look wildly different, and unaugmented and augmented forms (i.e., forms without *ro* and with *ro* respectively) could look quite unalike. McCone gives some lovely examples of this on pages 153 and 154 of his Grammar, including the extreme forms of *do-sluindi* 'denies': pret. 3 pl. *do-sluindset, -díltset*, perf/augm.pret. *do-ríltiset*,[45] *-derlaindset*.

Things were slightly simpler in those cases where the verbal stem began with a vowel. In those instances, *ro* simply dropped the vowel *o*.[46] This meant that *ro* did not count as an extra syllable, and as a result there was no additional syncope taking place. For example, *do-eim* 'protects', had a preterite *do-ét*, 'he protected', and a perfect (or, if you prefer, augmented preterite) *do-rét*. McCone refers to this *ro* as **prevocalic** (= standing before a vowel). Note that the prevocalic *ro* just happens to also be preverbal in this instance (in other words, *ro* stands directly before the verbal form) – you

---

you probably know, in Old Irish compound verbs, you could have multiple preverbs (an example of this is *fo-opair*, 'attacks' consisting of the preverbs *fo* and *uss* and the verbal stem *–ber*). These preverbs always stood in a particular order. Kim McCone gives a very handy overview in his book *The early Irish verb*, on p. 90, that I will give here as well (Stifter also gives it on p. 254 of his grammar):

1	2	3	4	5
to	*for*	*ad*	*cum*	*uss*
	fris	*ath(e)*	**ro**	*ne*
	eter	*ar(e)*		
	imb(e)	*de/dī*		
	ess			
	fo			
	in(de)			

This means that, theoretically speaking, if you wanted to create the preterite 3 sg. a compound verb of *beirid* with a stem *-bert* and the preverbs *ar*, *ne* and *to*, following the above overview, *to* would come first, followed by *ar* and finally *ne* (so **to-ar-ne-bert*), and also, that if you wished to change this into an augmented form, *ro* would be placed before *ne* (**to-ar-ro-ne-bert*). If *ro* preceded the preverbal particle *uss*, the two particles would be contracted to *róss, rúass*.

[45] The expected form would have been **do-roltaiset* – see Stifter: 255.

[46] McCone: 154.

could actually refer to this *ro* as **preverbal prevocalic *ro*** if you really wanted to. If you are really geeky, you can combine the two: prevercalic *ro*? Prevocerbal *ro*? Hmm. Maybe not.

Stage II.
Since forms like *do-rét* looked much more like their unaugmented counterparts (i.e. the forms without *ro*), it is not all that surprising that this started to spread to other compound verbs as well. The principle of putting *ro* before a vowel so you could get rid of the *o* and avoid syncope was therefore taken up by verbs that had a verbal stem beginning with a consonant, but that had a **stressed preverbal particle beginning in a vowel** (like *ar, eter, in, uss* in the prototonic form of the verb). The *ro* was now inserted before that vowel. This sounds very complicated, but let me give you an example – that might make it easier.

Take *do-immchella* (**to-imb-cell-*), 'goes around', *ní timchella*, with preterite 3 sg. **do-imchell, -timchell*. Originally, in the augmented form, you would have found **preverbal *ro***, in this case *do-immerchell* (**to-imb-**ro**-cell*). That is your regular preverbal *ro* right before the verb – nothing strange about it.

Now with the spread of **prevocalic *ro***, you start to find new forms where the *r* was placed **before the stressed preverb** beginning in a vowel, and you begin to see *do-rimchell* (**to-**ro**-imb-cell*) instead of *do-immerchell* (**to-imb-**ro**-cell*). This placement of *ro* before the stress(ed vowel) - you can call it **pretonic prevocalic *ro*** if you like - corresponds more or less to Thurneysen's **movable *ro*** (*GOI* §527).

Eventually, this whole system was simplified even further, and *ro* came to be treated as a conjunct particle that could be combined with other conjunct particles, so instead of for example *anaid*, preterite 3 sg. *anacht*, perf/augm. pret. *ro anacht, -ranacht*, you would start to see *ro anacht, níro anacht*, with *ro* attached to the conjunct particle *ní* rather than to the verbal form. Did you get all that? If not, don't panic. Let it sink in and read it again in a day or two.

Just to recap, here is the development of the placement of *ro*:

(1) **Preverbal *ro*** comes immediately before the verb (≈'fixed *ro*'), e.g. *do-intarrai*. If the verb begins in a vowel, *ro* loses the *o* and stands in front of it. This is called **(preverbal) prevocalic *ro*** : *do-rét*.

(2) **(Preverbal) prevocalic *ro*** leads to *ro* being moved in front of stressed preverbal particles beginning in a vowel, in other words: **(pretonic) prevocalic *ro*** (≈'movable *ro*'): *do-rintai*

(3) Over time, *ro* becomes a **conjunct particle** that can attach to other conjunct particles like *ní*, so *ro anacht*, *níro anacht* rather than earlier *ro anacht*, *ní ranacht*

Augmenting particles used instead of *ro*

(*GOI*: §§532-6; Lehmann: 71; McCone: 157-8; Quin: lesson 40; Stifter: 253; Strachan: -; Tigges: -)

Not all preterites are augmented (or turned into a perfect) by using the particle *ro*. In some cases, we find other preverbs. The most common of these are (for yet others, see for example *GOI* §534):

Use of *ad* instead of *ro*
In compounds with *com-*, most verbs beginning with a consonant have *ad* where you would normally expect *ro* to be.

Use of *com* instead of *ro*
Some important verbs, most (but not all) of them with roots ending in –*g*, have *com* infixed before the verbal stem. Examples of this: compounds of *orgaid* 'slays', but also compounds of –*ren* 'buys'. More examples can be found in *GOI* §533.

VII.g.4. Verbal adjective (past participle)

(*GOI*: §714-16; Lehmann: - ; McCone: 109; Quin: lesson 40; Stifter: 238; Strachan: 67-8; Tigges: 124-5)

The past participle is basically the word you use in English, in combination with 'to have', to express the perfect tense, e.g. 'killed', 'slain', 'woken', 'caught' etc. In Irish, this usually ends in –*the*. Like we saw in the preterite passive, if this comes after a guttural, you will get –*chte*; with verbs with a verbal root ending in a dental or *s*, the *th* changes to an *s*, as in *guidid* becoming *gesse* 'prayed'; with verbs with a root ending in a nasal, you get -*éte* (as in *canaid*, 'sings', *céte* 'sung', etcetera). The verbal adjective is declined like an *io,iā*-stem.

139

VII.g.5. Verbal of necessity (gerundive)
(*GOI*: §717-19; Lehmann:- ; McCone: 109; Quin: lesson 40; Stifter: - ; Strachan: 67-8; Tigges: 125-6)

This is used to express necessity, e.g. 'the criminal is to be hung' (i.e. must be hung), 'the songs are to be sung' etc.; it is indeclinable, and ends in – *th(a)i*, subject to the color of the final consonant of the verbal root. Don't worry too much about the verbal of necessity and the verbal adjective – they don't occur all that often. Just know that they exist for now.

VII.g.6. The verbal noun
(*GOI*: §§720--37; Lehmann: 13-14, 19, 70-1, 118-19, 123; McCone: - ; Quin: lesson 12; Stifter: 137-9; Strachan: - ; Tigges: 137-9)

As the name already suggests, the verbal noun is a noun formed from the verb. Since Old Irish does not have an infinitive (an infinitive is the form used to express the entire verb; English infinitives are 'to be', 'to walk', 'to go', 'to swim' etc.), the verbal noun can sometimes be used to express that.

The verbal noun, which you will encounter often if not very often, is considered a noun, so like all other nouns it has a certain gender and stem and it can come in different cases. Verbal nouns come in a large variety, so it is probably best to learn the gender and the stem for each verbal noun as you go along translating.

The verbal nouns of weak verbs of the *marbaid* and *léicid* kind often end in – *ad* or –*(i)ud* added to the stem of the verb. The verbal nouns that end in -*ad*/-*(i)ud* like that are usually *u*-stems masculine. Some examples of verbal nouns: the verb *marbaid*, 'kills' has a verbal noun *marbad* (with –*ad* added to the verbal stem to form the noun), *léicid*, 'allows', has *léiciud* as verbal noun; the verb *guidid*, prays, has as verbal noun *guide*, a feminine *iā*-stem.

The basic meaning of the verbal noun is 'the act of' followed by the meaning of the verb that formed the basis for the verbal noun, so *marbad* can be translated as 'the act of killing', *léiciud* as 'the act of allowing', *guide* as 'the act of praying' or 'prayer'.

There are a few **special constructions** used with the verbal noun. I will mention two constructions here that are important for you to remember:

(1) When you deal with a verbal noun, the **object** (so the person undergoing the action expressed in the verbal noun) is expressed by the **genitive case**. Because the genitive expresses the object, this is called an **objective genitive**. The agent, that is, the person who performs the action expressed by the verbal noun, is expressed by the preposition *do*. For example: *marbad ind eich don macc*: 'the killing of the horse by the boy', i.e. the boy kills the horse. One other example, that is often used to demonstrate this: *serc Dé dond ingin*: the love of (= for!) God by the girl, i.e. the girl's love for God and NOT 'the love of God for the girl'!

(2) The second construction is used to express an **act in progress** (the English *–ing* forms), like *stealing the car, buying the candy, building the house, singing the song* etc. To put it into a formula: this is the construction you will use to express *x-ing the y*. If you translate this into Irish, it looks like **at (the) x-ing of the y** (so if you would be translating sentences from English into Irish, you would be translating: 'at (the) stealing of the horse', 'at (the) buying of the candy', 'at (the) building of the house', 'at the singing of the song' etc.). In Old Irish they express this by using the preposition *oc* ('at', which causes no mutations and is followed by a word in the dative) **+ verbal noun in the dative** (because of *oc*; this verbal noun lenites the following word if it can because the dative singular always lenites) **+ genitive**: *oc marbad ind eich*, 'at the killing of the horse / killing the horse', *oc guidi Dé* 'at the beseeching of God / beseeching God', *oc tabairt óir* 'at bringing of gold / bringing gold' etc. For those of you who know Modern Irish: in Modern Irish the construction is the same; they use the modern equivalent of the preposition *oc*, the preposition *ag*: *ag déanamh, ag imirt*, etc. This construction is **very** common in Old Irish.

This brings us to the end of the chapter on the verb. I'm sure it may not always have been easy, so congratulations on having finished it!

VIII. RELATIVE CLAUSES

(*GOI*: §492-511.; Lehmann: 6, 29, 77-8; McCone: 41, 48-9, 67, 94-101; Quin: lessons 14, 32; Stifter: 165-70, 244-6; Strachan: 35-8; Tigges: 32, 132-6)

This brings us to an extremely important section – that of the relative clauses. I could have placed it earlier on among the verbal stems, but I think it is so important it needs its own chapter.

All of the sentences we have seen so far are regular sentences like 'the man walks, I see the island, a horse is killed, my bicycle is green.' This kind of sentence is called a **main clause**. But now you are ready for a different type of sentence. Look at the sentence 'I see the man who walks on the street.' This sentence is different from the ones above: it contains a **relative clause**. The relative clause gives you more information about the main clause. The relative clause usually starts with 'who, what, which, whom' and so on. This all sounds fairly complicated, so let me demonstrate:

I see the man **who walks on the street**

In this sentence, the part 'who walks on the street' gives you additional information about 'the man'. 'Who walks on the street' is therefore the relative clause. Relative clauses cannot stand on their own, they need something that they refer back to or give you information about. Let me give you another example.

The woman, **who is standing over there**, is smoking a cigar.

In this case, 'the woman…is smoking a cigar' is the main clause, and 'who is standing over there' is the relative clause. The relative clause here gives you more information about 'the woman'.

> The element that the relative clause refers back to or gives you additional information about is called the **antecedent**.

In the sentence 'I see the man who walks on the street', 'the man' is the antecedent, because that is the element in the main clause about which the relative clause gives you more information. In the sentence 'the woman, who is standing over there, is smoking a cigar', the antecedent is 'the woman.'

Are you still with me? Good. Now, let us take this one step further. In the sentence 'the woman, who is standing over there, is smoking a cigar', the element 'the woman' is the subject of the main clause 'the woman...is smoking a cigar'. Right?

Now, the same element, 'the woman' is also the subject of the relative clause. This is really easy to figure out if you make a new main clause from the relative clause: 'who is standing over there', replacing 'who' with the antecedent – this gives you 'the woman is standing over there'. Can you see that? Excellent. When this happens, we say that the antecedent ('the woman') stands in **subject-relation** to the relative clause.

I hope you are still following me. There is more. And this is a little tricky, so pay close attention:

The function of the antecedent in the main clause **does not have to be the same** as the function that it has in the relative clause.

I can make this clearer by looking at the first sentence I gave you:

'I see the man who walks on the street'

The **main clause** is: 'I see the man'
The **relative clause** is: 'who walks on the street'
The relative clause gives you more information about 'the man', therefore 'the man' is the **antecedent**.

Now, the important thing is to look at the element 'the man'. In the main clause, 'I see the man', the man is clearly the direct object. You all know this, I know you do!

If you look at the relative clause (replace the word 'who' with the antecedent for a second, which gives you 'the man walks on the street'), you can see that 'the man' serves as the subject of the relative clause; in other words, the antecedent stands in **subject-relation** to the relative clause, just like the sentence before did. So the **direct object of the main clause** is the antecedent, and stands in **subject-relation** to the relative clause.

If this is unclear in any way, ask someone to explain it again, because it is really important that you get this. As you may have guessed already, the antecedent does not always stand in subject-relation to the relative clause. It can also stand in **object-relation** to the relative clause, for example. Here are some examples of sentences in which the antecedent stands in object-relation to the relative clause; in all of these, the antecedent is in bold, and the relative clause in italics:

> **The man** *whom I see* walks down the street.
> I buy **the horse** *which you got for your birthday*
> **The warrior** *whom I admire most* has fallen in battle
> I talk to **the girl** *whom you know from school*

If you want to check if I am telling the truth about this object-relation thing, replace the *whom/which* with the antecedent, e.g. in the second line: 'the horse which you got' becomes 'you got the horse' – and in that sentence, the horse is clearly the direct object.

If the sentence stands in either of these relations (subject- or object-relation), it was considered to be a relative clause in Old Irish; but if the antecedent stood in any other relation (i.e., not in subject-/object-relation, like 'the guy **with whom** I went to school was just arrested'), the sentence was not considered a relative clause. For now, let's concentrate on the ones that were considered relative clauses, and look at what we find in Old Irish.

Note: I will not discuss genitival relation in this book (e.g. 'I see the man **whose** courage is failing him to learn Old Irish') as it does not occur all that often; for more information, see *GOI* §507 and Liam Breatnach's article in *Ériu* 31 (1980) 1-9.

VIII.a. Special relative verbal forms
(*GOI*: §493 and see under present indicative, present subjunctive, future, preterite active/passive for forms, mainly §§556, 558, 570, 576, 598, -601, 603, 620, 622, 638, 640, 663, 674, 684, 712, 738 ff; Lehmann: 77; McCone: 94-5; Quin: lesson 14; Stifter: 165-70; Strachan: listed under different paradigms from p. 35 onward; Tigges: 32-3, 152-9)

Old Irish has a few special forms of the verb that are used for relative clauses. **These special relative forms are always absolute.** This means that they are **only found with simple verbs**, and only if the forms are independent, i.e. not preceded by a conjunct particle, like *ní* or *in*. This also means that they are not found for those tenses/moods that use the secondary endings, as those are always preceded by a conjunct particle (in other words, you cannot have a special relative form in the imperfect indicative, past subjunctive or conditional).

All you need to do in order to put a verb in a relative form is to add the relative ending you want to the stem of the verb. The special forms of the relative are pretty much the same for all tenses and moods that can take the relative (i.e. present indicative, present subjunctive, future, (unaugmented) preterite active/passive). There are not even special relative forms for each person, only for the third person singular and the first and third person plural in the active, and for the 3 sg. and 3 pl. in the passive. This is the pattern:

3 sg. active	*-as/-es*
1 pl. active	*-m(a)e*
3 pl. active	*-t(a)e*
3 sg. passive	*-thar/ther* or *—ar* after verbs from the *beirid-* (BI) or *benaid-*group (BIV)
3 pl. passive	*-tar/-ter*

Here are some examples of the special forms in the present indicative:

in fer **beires** *in claideb*	'the man who carries the sword'
in fer **beires** *in macc*	'the man who carries the boy' *or*
	'the man whom the boy carries'
in claideb **bermae**	'the sword which we carry'
in claideb **bertae**	'the sword which they carry'
in claideb **berar**	'the sword which is carried'
in maicc **bertar**	'the boys who are carried'

If you want to apply these forms to other tenses, just make sure you are using the correct stem and remember that you may find an extra letter (e.g., the relative forms in the *s*-subjunctive will usually show the letter *s*, consisting of stem + *s* + relative ending). Let me show you some examples of what the relatives would look like with the verb *marbaid* 'kills', *beirid* 'carries', *téit* 'goes' and *cingid* 'steps' (since they have different kinds of subjunctives and preterites):

		pres. ind.	pres. subj.	future	pret. act.
Active					
Sg.	3.	*marbas*	*marbas*	*mairbfes*	*marbas*
Pl.	1.	*marbmae*	*marbmae*	*mairbfimme*[47]	?
Pl.	3.	*marbtae/*	*marbtae/*	*mairbfite*	*marbsaite*
		marbaite	*marbaite*		
Passive					
Sg.	3.	*marbthar*	*marbthar*	*mairbfider*	– [48]
Pl.	3.	*marb(a)tar*	*marb(a)tar*	*mairbfiter*	–

---

[47] There is an extra vowel here to make the word pronouncable.

[48] Remember that you have special forms for the preterite passive!

		pres. ind.	pres. subj.	future	pret. act
Active					
Sg.	3.	*beires*	*beras*	*béras*	*bertae*
Pl.	1.	*bermae*	*bermae*	*bérmae*	?
Pl.	3.	*bertae*	*bertae*	*bértae*	*bertatar*
Passive					
Sg.	3.	*berar*	*berthar*	*bérthar*	-
Pl.	3.	*bertar*	*bertar*	*bértar*	-

		pres. ind.	pres. subj.	future	pret. act.
Active					
Sg.	3.	*téite*	*tías*	*regas*	*luide*
Pl.	1.	*tíagmae*	*tíasmae*	*regmae*	?
Pl.	3.	*tíagtae*	*tíastae*	*regtae*	?
Passive					
Sg.	3.	*tíagar*	*tías(t)ar*	*regthar*	-
Pl.	3.	*tíagtar*	*tíasatar*	*regtar*	-

		pres. ind.	pres. subj.	future	pret. act
Active					
Sg.	3.	*cinges*	*cías*	*ciches*	?
Pl.	1.	*cingmae*	*cíasmae*	*cichsimme*	?
Pl.	3.	*cengtae*	*cíastae*	*cichsite*	?
Passive					
Sg.	3.	*cengar*	*cías(t)ar*	*cichsither*	?
Pl.	3.	*cengtar*	*cíasatar*	*cichsiter*	?

The only difference is found in some of the relative forms of the preterite active where you find the endings –*(a)e* and *(ta)tar* in the singular and plural respectively.

Deponent verbs also have the five relative forms:

3 sg. deponent	*-athar/ -ethar/ -edar*
1 pl. deponent	*-ammar/ -emmar/-mer*
3 pl. deponent	*-atar/ -etar*
3 sg. passive	*-thar/ -ther*
3 pl. passive	*-tar/ -ter*

It may be overkill, but just to make sure you understand: the special forms are only used when possible in those sentences that **in Irish** are felt to be relative (remember the whole subject-/object-relation thing?). In all other cases, you use regular verbal forms. Look below in the section 'cleft sentences' (VIII.f.) for some examples.

VIII.b. Leniting relative clauses
(*GOI*: §§ 494-96; Lehmann: 77; McCone: 95-6; Quin: lesson 14; Stifter: 169-70; Strachan: - ; Tigges: 132-3, 142)

Now for the obvious question: what do you do for the other persons for which you don't have the special forms? Well, it depends a little bit on the relation of the antecedent with the relative clause. Basically, for the other persons, you take the conjunct form of the verb (if there is no conjunct particle, you use the particle *no*) and you lenite the first letter of the verbal form. This relative clause is therefore called a **leniting relative clause** (makes sense, right, because the first letter of the verb is lenited). This gives us the following pattern, with the persons that have special forms between brackets for the sake of being complete:

1 sg.	*In lebor no chrenaim*	'the book that I buy'
2 sg.	*In lebor nád chrenai*	'the book that you don't buy'
(3 sg.	*in lebor c(h)renas*	'the book that he buys')
(1 pl.	*in lebor c(h)renmae*	'the book that we buy')
2 pl.	*in lebor nád chrenaid*	'the book that you do not buy'
(3 pl.	*in lebor c(h)rentae*	'the book that they buy')

In texts, you'll often find the initials of the special relative forms lenited, even though that is not strictly necessary; that is why I have put the lenition here between brackets.

> The leniting relative clause **has to be used** when the antecedent stands in **subject-relation** to the relative clause, and it **is optional** when the antecedent stands in **object-relation**.

For those of you who are too curious for your own good: when the antecedent stands in object-relation, you can also use a **nasalising relative clause** (you have to choose between the two). The nasalising relative clause looks pretty much the same as the leniting relative clause, except that instead of lenition, you get nasalization, e.g. *in claideb no-mbiur*, 'the sword which I carry'. It will be discussed more extensively below in its own section.

I have mentioned before that the special relative forms are only found with the absolute forms of the verb. This means that this always involves simple verbs. If the verb you are dealing with is a **compound verb**, or if it is found in a **conjunct form** or in a secondary tense, it does not have special forms. In that case, you just use the regular form of the verb and infix the lenition, like *in fer ad-chí in n-ech* 'the man who sees the horse.' In this sentence, you can see that you are dealing with a relative clause for two reasons:

(1) the verb *ad-cí* is lenited (*ad-**chí***)
(2) the verb is **not** in the position in which you would normally expect to find it: in a regular main clause, the verb stands first. The verb in a relative clause almost always comes **after the antecedent**.

Some other important points:

When you wish to put a relative clause in the negative, you do NOT use the particle *ní*; you use the conjunct particle ***nád***; this is of course followed by lenition in a leniting relative clause: *in fer **nád cheil** in macc*, 'the man who does not hide the boy', or 'the man whom the boy does not hide'; *ad-cí in fer in macc **nád cheil** a n-ór*, 'the man sees the boy who does not hide the gold' (in the case of a nasalizing relative clause, it is of course followed by nasalization).

Needless to say, after the conjunct particle *nád*, you will NEVER find the special relative forms.

VIII.c. Nasalizing relative clauses
(*GOI*: §§497-504; Lehmann: 77; McCone: 98-9; Quin: lesson 32; Stifter: 244-6; Strachan: - ; Tigges: 133-6, 143)

It is now time to ~~meet your doom~~ look more closely at the nasalizing relative clause. The nasalizing relative clause can occur in a number of different situations; the most common ones will be discussed in this section.

First, let me repeat when exactly you use a leniting relative clause:

A leniting relative clause **must** be used when the antecedent stands in **subject-relation** to the relative clause, e.g. *I see the man who lives next to me.*

A leniting relative clause **may** also be used when the antecedent stands in **object-relation** to the relative clause, e.g. *I see the girl whom I love.*

In the second case, that where the antecedent stands in object-relation, you can also use a **nasalizing relative clause**, as said above. In a nasalizing relative clause, where possible, nasalization is shown before the first letter of the simple verb, or before the stressed element in a compound verb:

Simple verb
absolute:
*Ad-cí in claideb **m**beires cosin cath*
'she sees the sword which he carries to the battle'

conjunct:
*Fo-gaibim in claideb nád **m**beir cosin cath*
'I seize the sword which he does not carry to the battle'

Compound verb
deuterotonic:
*Ad-cí in claideb do-**m**beir cosin cath*
'she sees the sword which he brings to the battle'

prototonic:
*Do-gní a n-í nád **n**dénaid,*
'he does that which you (pl.) do not do'

Note: This is slightly different when dealing with the copula. If a sentence occurs with a relative form of the copula, like *as* pres. ind. 3 sg. 'who is' and *ata* pres. ind. 3 pl. 'who are' the copula itself is not mutated, but the initial of the **following stressed word** is (usually, this is the predicate). See the following examples from the Workbook: *hóre as **n**-úasal in lóech* 'because the warrior is noble', *céin as **m**béo:* 'as long as he is alive'.

If there is no special relative form (i.e. when dealing with the 1 and 2 persons of the copula), you need to use the coat-rack particle *no*, just like with any other verb. In that case, mutations *are* shown at the beginning of the copula because *no* itself is unstressed, e.g. *amal no-n-da thorisse* 'as I am trustworthy' (Wb. 10a28).

VIII.d. Other uses for the nasalizing relative clause
(*GOI*: §§497-504; Lehmann: 77; McCone: 98-9; Quin: lesson 32; Stifter: 244-6; Strachan: - ; Tigges:135-6)

The nasalizing relative clause is found on a number of other occasions, namely:

A. When the antecedent is the verbal noun of the verb in the relative clause.
This is also called the **figura etymologica**. This construction is fairly common. In English, this would be something like 'to smile a smile', 'to laugh a laugh', 'to drink a drink'. An example of this occurs in the infamous gloss 25 in Strachan's *Paradigms* (Ml. 102a15: *ar is cuit* **adaill ad-n-ellat-sidi**... 'for it is a mere passing visit with which they visit…').

B. If an adjective is the antecedent, and it is used in an adverbial sense
This sounds very complicated, I know. It is actually not that difficult. It just means that the antecedent of the relative clause is an adjective ('good', 'bad', 'blue', 'diligent'), and it gives you information about how the action in the relative clause is accomplished, e.g. *is dían do-n-eccat ind eich* 'it is swiftly that the horses come', with the adjective *dían* 'swift' as the antecedent. Thurneysen actually places this under the section of the antecedent indicating the manner in which or to what extent the action of the relative clause is done (*GOI* §498), see C.2. below.

C. After conjunctions consisting of nouns or pronouns
This category can be further divided:

C.1. It can be used when the antecedent denotes a **time** at or during which the action in the relative clause takes place (e.g. 'at the time you were eating'). This then extends to temporal conjunctions, like *in tan* 'when', *céin* 'as long as', *a* 'when', *lasse* 'while', and *óre* 'because' (this may seem out of place, but this is actually the genitive of *úar*, 'hour')

C.2. It can be used when the antecedent gives you the **manner** in which or **extent** to which the action of the relative clause is done (i.e. 'that is the extent to which it has been done'). This then also starts to occur after conjunctions such as *amal* 'as', and *feib* 'as'.

C.3. The nasalizing relative clause is also found after an antecedent specifying the **reason** for the action in the relative clause, and then spreads to causal conjunctions like *fo bith* and *deg* 'because'.

D. To introduce indirect or reported speech

Indirect or reported speech means that someone else informs you of what has been said, as in 'he says **that he will go to the movies**' (Direct speech in a text is for example 'he says: 'I will go to the movies''). Obviously, this means that this construction is used after verbs of saying. It also occurs after verbs of thinking 'he thought that he would like to go to the movies', and after expressions such as 'it happens, it is clear that...' (*GOI* §503). An example given in the Workbook, lesson 32: *as-berat* **do-ngníat** *deg-gnímu* 'they say that they do good deeds.'

E. the antecedent expresses the concept that constitutes the predicative nominative of the relative clause (as Thurneysen put it in *GOI* §500), e.g. *cid drúailnide m-bes chechtar in da rann*, Sg. 202b3, literally 'although it is corrupt that each of the two parts be'. Again, this sounds very complicated, but think of it this way: if you were to rephrase this sentence, in a normal main clause, you would get 'although each of the two parts is corrupt', and here you can clearly see that 'corrupt' is the predicate of that clause. Thurneysen here includes the construction *ol-dáu* etc. which appears after the comparative (see also section III.d.2 above).

VIII.e. Preposition followed by the relative particle *a*

(*GOI*: §492; Lehmann: - ; McCone: 41-2, 67, 94 ; Quin: lesson 32; Stifter: 261-2; Strachan: -; Tigges: 110)

The combination of preposition + relative particle $(s)a^n$ (e.g. *lasa* 'with which/whom', *fora* 'on which/whom') is not considered to be a relative construction in Old Irish (because the antecedent does not stand in subject or object relation to the relative clause). This means that it is NOT followed by a relative verbal form, but by a regular verbal form.

Basically, what you do is you take the preposition, and tack on the relative $(s)a$. The prepositions co^n and i^n are very tricky here, as the relative *a* disappears entirely, and you just see *co* or *i*. An example of this (and here you can clearly see that the construction preposition + relative *a* is NOT followed by the relative form of the verb) can be found in the following gloss (number 31 in the *Paradigms*, Wb. 3c2): *tri chretim i n-Ísu nó isin beothu* **i táa** *Ísu íar n-esséirgu* 'through belief in Jesus, or in the life **in which Jesus is** after resurrection'.

VIII.f. Cleft sentences

GOI: §513 (on position of verb); Lehmann: 7, 27 (this is called 'marked constructions'); McCone: 47-9; Quin: - ; Stifter: 263 (section on fronting) ; Strachan: - ; Tigges: 134-5)

Earlier on in the book (in section V.a. on independent pronouns above), I brought up the term 'cleft sentence'. So what is a cleft sentence? A **cleft sentence** is a sentence that is re-organized so you can put a special **emphasis** on one of the different elements in that sentence. The element that is emphasized is **brought forward** to the beginning of the sentence. Let me give you an example – that might make it clearer.

Take the sentence: 'The man is writing a book in his house'

First, divide the sentence in different elements (subject, object etc.). The different elements are:

    'the man' (subject)
    'is writing' (verb)
    'a book' (object)
    'in his house' (adverbial part).

Now, you can pick any one of these elements and put special emphasis on it. In the following sentences I have highlighted the emphasized elements:

a.   It is **the man** who is writing a book in his house (and not the woman)
b.   It is **at the writing of a book** that the man is in his house   (he's not knitting a sweater)
c.   It is **a book** that the man is writing in his house (and not a   song)
d.   It is **in his house** that the man is writing a book (and not in the cinema)

As you can see, two things change when you bring an element forward in English to put more emphasis on it:
(1) you use a form of the copula at the beginning of the sentence.
(2) in English, the emphasized part is followed by a relative clause (it is the man who writes a book…)

That is good to know of course, but what about Old Irish? Well, in Old Irish this is mostly the same. Note that I say *mostly* – so not completely. So what is different? The first change is the same:

152

> The sentence will start with a form of the copula, followed by the element that you want to emphasize.

The difference lies in the second change:

> In Old Irish, the emphasized part of the sentence is ONLY followed by a **relative clause** if the part brought forward is the **subject or direct object** of the sentence.
>
> It is NOT followed by a relative clause if the element brought forward is NOT the subject or direct object. Instead, you will find the regular verbal form.

Let me show you by giving you an example. Take the Old Irish sentence: *beirid int ech in fer cosin n-insi* ('the horse carries the man to the island'). The elements here are:

beirid	(verb part – remember, the normal word order in Old Irish is verb-subject-*o*bject!)
int ech	(subject)
in fer	(direct object)
cosin n-insi	(adverbial part)

Now, as I just said, in Old Irish, in order to put emphasis on a part you bring it forward, you add a form of the copula and, if the element that is brought forward is the subject or object, you use a relative clause. If the element is not the subject or the object (so in our case this goes for the verb and for the adverbial part), you do not get a relative clause. And another thing: if you bring **the verb** forward, you have to use a special combination of the preposition *oc* + verbal noun + genitive (described above in the verb chapter, section VII.g.6). Let's take a look:

1. *Is **int ech beires** in fer cosin n-insi*
   'It is **the horse** that carries the man to the island'
2. *Is **in fer beires** int ech cosin n-insi*
   'It is **the man** whom the horse carries to the island'
3. *Is **cosin n-insi beirid** int ech in fer*
   'It is **to the island** that the horse carries the man'
4. *Is **oc breth ind fir cosin n-insi attá** int ech,*
   literally giving us the phenomenally awful-sounding translation 'It is **at the carrying of the man to the island** that the horse is.'

153

People also call the type of sentence in which the **subject** is brought forward (sentence number 1 above) a **cleft I** ('cleft one') sentence.

The type of sentence in which the **direct object** is brought forward (sentence number 2 above) is referred to as a **cleft II** ('cleft two') sentence.

Sentences in which **other parts** are brought forward for emphasis are usually called **cleft III** ('cleft three') sentences. You can see that these sentences have a regular verbal form (*attá* and *beirid* respectively). So remember:

Only **cleft I** and **cleft II** make use of the relative clause after the element that has been brought forward. **Cleft III** sentences are *not* followed by a relative clause, but by regular verbal forms.

IX. THE VERBS 'TO BE':
COPULA AND SUBSTANTIVE VERB

In Old Irish (and indeed in Modern Irish still) there are two verbs to express the English verb 'to be': the **substantive verb** and the **copula**. Now when do you use which? The verbs for 'to be' often occur in sentences of the type 'X is Y'. In this sentence type, X is the subject of the sentence, and Y is what is known as the **predicate**. The basic rule in Old Irish is this:

The **copula** is used when the predicate is a noun, an adjective or a pronoun.
The **substantive verb** is used when the predicate is something else.

An easy way to figure out if you need to use a copula is by taking the predicate as the answer to a question. The copula is used for questions of the type 'X is who/what? (X being the subject)'; the substantive verb is used for questions of the type 'X is where/doing what?' Allow me to demonstrate.

Let us take the following sentence: 'Conn is king'. In this sentence, 'Conn' is the subject of the sentence, 'is' is the verb, and 'king' is the predicate. If you turn this statement into a question, you will get 'What is Conn?' – the answer, of course, is 'king'. Since the question you have asked is of the type 'X is who/what?', you will expect to find a **copula** in the Old Irish version of this sentence. Indeed you do, as the outcome in Old Irish is *is rí Conn*. Other examples of sentences where you would find the copula are sentences like 'the house is big', 'the weather is awful' and 'Cú Chulainn is the most awesome warrior in the history of earth'.

Note that the word-order in these sentences with the copula is slightly different from the one you are used to – the 'regular' word-order is verb-subject-object (remember?), but here it is **copula-predicate-subject**. Many people think that something funny is going on, but I assure you that this is the NORMAL word-order.

Another example. Take the sentence 'I am reading this book'. The subject of the sentence is 'I', followed by the verb 'am'; 'reading this book' is the predicate of the sentence. Now turn this into a question, and what do you get? Exactly: 'I am doing what?' – this means that in Old Irish, the substantive verb should be used, and, lo and behold! It is: *at-tó* (remember that 'I' is here included in the verbal ending) *oc légund ind libuir-se* (lit. 'I am at (the) reading of this book').

This is a construction often found with verbal nouns (see also above, section VII.g.6): substantive verb + *oc* 'at' + verbal noun in the dative (since *oc* is followed by a dative case) + whatever else is included. *Oc* + verbal noun roughly corresponds to the English –ing form ((I am) walk**ing**, sing**ing**, pray**ing**, skat**ing** etc.). Other instances for the use of the substantive are 'Conn is here', 'I am in the big red barn' etc. (in these examples the predicates provide the answers to the questions 'Where is Conn?' and 'Where am I?' respectively).

I hope it has become a little bit clearer to you when which verb 'to be' is used. Now let's look at the different forms of these two verbs. I am going to start by looking at the copula.

IX.a. The copula
(*GOI*: §§791-818; Lehmann: 15, 53-5, 94, 105-6; McCone: 39-40, 43-5, 48-9; Quin: lesson 15; Stifter: 119-21, 180, 218-9, 276, 294-5, 386 (whole paradigm); Strachan: 72-3; Tigges: 44, 46, 62, 78, 88, 98, 101, 111, 122, 134, 152)

Before I give you the pattern, I want to direct your attention to some Very Important Points (V.I.P.s) about the copula:

(1) I have just said this, but it is important so I am saying it again: you know that the normal word order in regular sentences is VSO, but not in copula sentences, nosiree. The regular word order in copula sentences is **copula-predicate-subject**. Beware of this when you are translating sentences!

(2) The conjunct forms of the copula are usually attached to the conjunct particle. **The third person singular conjunct has no ending; it looks exactly like the conjunct particle**. This means for example that the interrogative particle *in*, combined with the copula 3 sg. conjunct is also *in*. In the same way, *ní* + 3 sg. conjunct of the copula is also *ní* and the relative negation *nád* (only used in relative sentences) + 3 sg. conjunct of the copula is *nád*. So be on your guard when you translate a text: the word *ní* can either mean 'not' or 'is not'. Obviously, if the word *ní* is followed by a conjunct or prototonic verbal form it has to be the regular negative particle *ní* meaning 'not'.

(3) Since the predicate gives you information about the subject of the sentence, and the subject of a sentence stands in the nominative case, **the predicate has to correspond in form to the subject, if the predicate is a noun or adjective.** This means that if the subject stands in the nominative singular, the noun or adjective forming the predicate will also stand in the nominative singular. If the subject stands in the nominative plural, the predicate will stand in the nominative plural if it is a noun or adjective.

(4) The copula is **unstressed.** Instead, **the word following it will receive the stress.** So if you take the sentence *is rí in fer* 'the man is a king', the stress falls on *rí*, and NOT on *is*!

IX.a.1. Present stem

Present indicative
The forms of the copula, present indicative:

		Absolute	Conjunct
Sg.	1.	*am*	*-ta, -da*
	2.	*at or it*	*-ta, -da*
	3.	*is*	none – it is absorbed into the conjunct particle.
Pl.	1.	*ammi*	*-tan, -dan*
	2.	*adib*	*-tad, -dad*
	3.	*it*	*-tat, -dat*

Here is an example of the conjunct forms of the copula present indicative attached to the conjunct particle *ní* (make sure also to check out the other possibilities in for example Strachan's *Paradigms* pp. 72-3):

Sg.	1.	*níta, nída* (lenites the following word if it can) 'I am not'
	2.	*níta* (lenites the following word if it can) 'you are not'
	3.	*ní* (!) 'he/she is not'
Pl.	1.	*nítan, nídan* (lenites the following word if it can) 'we are not'
	2.	*nítad, nídad* 'you are not'
	3.	*níta(a)t, nídat* 'they are not'

The forms that are most common (this goes for every verb, really) are those in the third person singular and the third person plural.

Here are some sentences using the absolute forms given above:

Am rechtaire	'I am a steward'
At becc	'You are small'
Is rí in fer	'The man is a king'
Ammi rígnai	'We are queens'
Adib sacairt	'You are priests'
It amrai ind eich	'The horses are wonderful'

The copula also has relative forms. The forms that are found in extant texts (or, to use a fancy word, the forms that are attested) are those of 3 sg. and 3 pl.:

Sg. 3. *as* 'who is'
　　　ad-cíu in fer **as** *rí*, 'I see the man who is king'
Pl. 3. *at(a)* 'who are'
　　　ad-cíu inna firu **ata** *ríg* 'I see the men who are kings'

In the negative:
Sg. 3. *nád* 'who is not'
　　　ad-cíu in fer **nád** *rí*, 'I see the man who is not king'
Pl. 3. *natat* 'who are not'
　　　ad-cíu inna firu **natat** *ríg* 'I see the men who are not kings'

These words lenite the following word (if they can) **if the antecedent stands in subject-relation to the relative clause** (in the above example, the antecedent *in fer* stands in subject-relation to the relative clause). All persons except the third persons have to use that coat-rack particle *no* discussed before, and are basically followed by the conjunct forms that we have already seen. Luckily, these forms hardly ever occur, so don't worry about them for now.

Imperfect indicative
The imperfect indicative of the copula looks exactly like the preterite – so you get two for the price of one!

		Absolute	**Conjunct**
Sg.	1.	*basa*	*-bsa/-psa*
	2.	*basa*	**-bsa/*-psa*
	3.	*ba*	*-bo/-po/-bu/-pu* (these four cause lenition)
Pl.	1.	**bamar*	**-bmar*
	2.	**bad*	?
	3.	*batar/batir*	*-btar/-ptar*

158

Imperative

Sg.	1.	-
	2.	*ba*
	3.	*bad/bed*
Pl.	1.	*ban*
	2.	*bad/bed*
	3.	*bat*

IX.a.2. Subjunctive stem

Present subjunctive

		Absolute	**Conjunct**
Sg.	1.	*ba*	*-ba* (lenites)
	2.	*ba/be*	*-ba*
	3.	*ba,*	*-bo/-p/-b* (and note the forms *cid*, *mad* 'although it be, if it be' respectively where the form of the copula is reduced to *-d*)
Rel.		*bes/bas* (lenites)	
Pl.	1.	**bammi*[49]	*-ban* (lenites)
	2.	*bede*	*-bad* (lenites?)
	3.	*bat*	*-pat* (lenites; also note the forms *cit*, *mat*)
Rel.		*bete/beta* (lenites)	

Past subjunctive

Sg.	1.	*−benn, -bin*
	2.	*-ptha*
	3.	*-bed/-bad/-bid* (note again the forms *cid/mad* 'although it were, if it were')
Pl.	1.	*-bemmis, -bimmis*
	2.	**-bede*
	3.	*-bitis/betis, -btis/-ptis* and note *cetis*, *matis*

IX.a.3. Future stem

Future

		Absolute	**Conjunct**
Sg.	1.	*be*	?
	2.	*be/ba*	?
	3.	*bid*	*-ba/-pa*

---

[49] In McCone: 43.

159

Rel.   *bes/bas*
Pl. 1. *bimmi/bemmi/bami*   ?
    2. *bethi(b)*[50]   ?
    3. *bit*   -bat
Rel.   *beta/bat*

Conditional
Sg. 1. ?
    2. ?
    3. *robad/bed/bad*
Pl. 1. ?
    2. ?
    3. *beitis/roptis*

IX.a.4. Preterite active stem

Preterite
As stated before, these forms are identical to the imperfect indicative:

		Absolute	**Conjunct**
Sg.	1.	*basa*	*-bsa/-psa*
	2.	*basa*	**-bsa/*-psa*
	3.	*ba*	*-bo/-po/-bu/-pu* (these four cause lenition)
Pl.	1.	**bamar*	?
	2.	**bad*	?
	3.	*batar/batir*	*-btar/-ptar*

Perfect
As expected by now, the preterite is formed (or the preterite is augmented) by combining *ro* with the conjunct forms of the preterite:

		Independent	**Dependent**
Sg.	1.	*ropsa/robsa*	*-rbsa*
	2.	*ropsa*	?
	3.	*ropo/robo/ropu/robu,*	*-rbo/-rbu*
Pl.	1.	*robummar*	*-rbommar*
	2.	?	?
	3.	*roptar/robtar*	*-rbtar*

---

[50] In McCone: 43.

IX.a.5. Other: verbal noun

The verbal noun of the substantive verb, *buith*, can also be used as the verbal noun for the copula – see *GOI* §817.

IX.b. The substantive verb *at-tá*

(*GOI*: §§774-789; Lehmann: 52-3, 105-6; McCone: 40-3, 49; Quin: lesson 12; Stifter: 133,136-7, 179-80, 218, 233, 294, 385 (complete paradigm); Strachan: 68-71; Tigges: 43-4, 46, 62, 71, 78, 88, 98, 101, 111, 122, 151-2)

The forms used in the regular present tense come from a hiatus verb with the stem *tá-*; the other tenses and moods are made with a different hiatus verb with a stem *bi-/be-*.

IX.b.1. Present stem

Present indicative

These are the regular forms of the substantive verb, present indicative:

1 sg. *at-tó* I am	1 pl. *at-taám*	we are
2 sg. *at-taí* you are	2 pl. *at-taáid*	you are
3 sg. *at-tá* he/she/it is	3 pl. *at-taát*	they are

The vowels *–aa-* in the plural are to be pronounced separately, so these words have three syllables rather than two (so *at-ta-am*).

After conjunct particles like *ní* and *in*, you use a special verbal form -*fil*. This form comes originally from a verb meaning 'to see', and basically means 'one sees' (but even though if you find the form *fil* in a text, you would always translate it as a form of the verb 'to be'). This form is **not conjugated** (in other words, it is the same for all persons). Here comes the important part:

The form *fil* is followed by the **accusative case**.

This may seem very odd at first, but if you know, as I just wrote, that the basic meaning of *fil* is 'one sees', it makes much more sense. Let us assume you want to say 'the horse is not here' in Old Irish. How do you go about this?

161

Well, obviously, first you figure out which of the two verbs 'to be' you need. Since the question answered is of the 'X is where?' type, you can see that you will need to use the substantive verb (this almost goes without saying of course, since I am explaining something relating to the substantive verb here).

Then you will hopefully see that there is a 'not' in the sentence and that since *ní* is a conjunct particle, you will need to use the form *fil*.

If you were to rewrite the sentence in your head using the 'one sees' meaning of *fil*, you will get: 'one does not see the horse here'. If you analyse that sentence, 'one' is the subject, 'does (not) see' is the verb, 'the horse' is **the direct object**, and 'here' is an adverbial designator. The outcome of this in Old Irish is therefore: *ní fil **in n-ech** sund*.

But what do we do when the object of this type of sentence is a personal pronoun (me, you, him, her, it, us, you or them)? This is very simple. We have already seen that whenever the object of a sentence is a personal pronoun, you have to use an **infixed pronoun**. The same applies here. Let me give you the paradigm (list) for the use of *fil* with infixed pronouns class A expressing the direct object after the conjunct particle *ní* (is everyone still with me?):

1 sg.	*ním-fil*	I am not (lit. 'one does not see **me**')
2 sg.	*nít-fil*	You are not (lit. 'one does not see **you**')
3 sg. masc.	*ní-fil*	He is not (lit. 'one does not see **him**')
3 sg. fem.	*nís-fil*	She is not (lit. 'one does not see **her**')
3 sg. neut.	*ní-fil*	It is not (lit. 'one does not see **it**')
1 pl.	*nín-fil*	We are not (lit. 'one does not see **us**')
2 pl.	*níb-fil*	You are not (lit. 'one does not see **you**')
3 pl.	*nís-fil*	They are not (lit. 'one does not see **them**')

Note the 3 sg. masculine and neuter – the infixed pronoun (*a*) has disappeared! In the case of 3 sg. neuter, you can at least see that something is going on because -*fil* is lenited. It is really important to remember that you can also use the infixed pronoun with the form –*tá* in order to express possession (infixed pronoun functions as the indirect object, 'to/for x')

I have already given you the paradigm of 'I have' etc: *táthum/ nom-thá* in the section on the pronouns, but for the sake of being complete, here it is again:

162

Sg.	1.	*nom-thá*	*táthum*	'There is to me' = I have
	2.	**not-tá*	*táthut*	You have
	3.m.	**na-tá*	*táthai*	He has
	3.f.	*nos-tá*	*táthus*	She has
	3.n.	**na-tá*	*táthai*	It has
Pl.	1.	*non-tá*	*táithiunn*	We have
	2.	*nob-tá*	*táthuib*	You (pl.) have
	3.	*nos-tá*	*táthus*	They have

The **relative form** of the substantive verb *at-tá* is *fil* or *file* if it is not preceded by a conjunct particle, and *fil* if it is: *in fer fil(e) sund; in fer nád fil sund.* 'the man who is here; the man who is not here'.

Apart from this, the substantive verb also has something called a **habitual present**. As the term implies, this expresses things that happen often (habitually). These forms are formed with the stem *bi-*. Here are the forms of the habitual present:

		Absolute	**Conjunct**	
Sg.	1.	*biuu,*	-*bíu*	'I am usually/I am wont to be'
	2.	**bii,*	-*bí*	'You are usually'
	3.	*biid,*	-*bí*	'He/She it is usually'
Rel.		*búis, bís*		'Who is usually'
Impers.		*bíthir-bíther, -*	*rubthar*	'One is usually'
Pl.	1.	*bimmi,*	-*biam*	'We are usually'
	2.	*bíthe,*	-*biid*	'You (pl.) are usually'
	3.	*biit*	-*biat*	'They are usually'
Rel.		*bite*		'Who are usually'

Imperfect indicative and imperative

Now for the two other tenses of the present stem: the imperfect indicative and the imperative. Again, the stem is *bi-* (no distinction between regular and habitual here!), and the endings are tacked on (this gives us **biinn* in the 1 sg. imperfect indicative, which becomes *bínn*, and so on for the other persons):

Imperfect indicative

Sg.	1.	-*bínn*
	2.	**-bítha*
	3.	-*bíth*
Impers.		-*bíthe*

Pl.	1.	*-bimmis*
	2.	*-*bíthe*
	3.	*-bítis*

Imperative

Sg.	1.	-
	2.	*bí*
	3.	*bíth*

Pl.	1.	*biam*
	2.	*biid*
	3.	*biat*

IX.b.2. Subjunctive stem

The subjunctive stem is *be-*, and the endings are added to that stem:

		Present subjunctive		Past subjunctive
		Absolute	**Conjunct**	
Sg.	1.	*béo/béu*	*-béo/-béu*	*-beinn*
	2.	*bé*	*-bé*	*-betha*
	3.	*beith*	*-bé*	*-beth*
Rel.		*bess*	---	---
Impers.		*bethir*		*-bethe*
Pl.	1.	*beimmi*	*-bem*	*-bemmis*
	2.	*beithe*	*-beith*	*-bethe*
	3.	*beit*	*-bet*	*-betis*
Rel.		*bete*	---	---

IX.b.3. Future stem

The forms of the conditional look exactly the same as the past subjunctive, except for the third person singular, so be careful with all other persons! Another thing to note is that the regular conjunct particle used with the substantive verb is **not *no*, but *ro***.

		Future		Conditional
		Absolute	**Conjunct**	
Sg.	1.	*bia*	*-*bi*	*-beinn*
	2.	*bie*	*-bie*	*-betha*
	3.	*bieid*	*-bia*	*-biad*
Rel.		*bias*	---	---
Imper.		*bethir*	*-bether*	*bethe

Pl.	1.	*bemmi*	*-biam*	*-bemmis*
	2.	*bethe*	*-bieid, -bied*	*-bethe*
	3.	*bieit*	*-biat*	*-betis*
Rel.		*bete*	---	---

IX.b.4. Preterite active stem

Preterite

The forms of the substantive verb follow more or less the same pattern as the endings of the reduplicated preterite, except that it ends in a vowel rather than a consonant; there is generally no distinction between absolute and conjunct, but we only have a conjunct form for the 2 pl.:

Sg.	1.	*bá*
	2.	*bá*
	3.	*boí/ baí*
Rel.		*boíe*
Impers.		*bothae, -both*
Pl.	1.	*bámmar*
	2.	*-baid*
	3.	*bátar/ bátir*

Perfect

For the perfect or augmented preterite, *ro* is simply placed before the forms:

		Independent	**Dependent**
Sg.	1.	*ro bá*	*-roba*
	2.	*ro bá*	*-roba, -raba*
	3.	*ro boí*	*-robae, -rabae*
Pl.	1.	*ro bámmar*	*-robammar*
	2.	*ro baid*	*-robaid*
	3.	*ro bátar*	*-robatar, -rabatar*

IX.b.5. Other: verbal of necessity, verbal noun

The verbal noun of *at-tá* is *buith* '(act of) being'; the verbal of necessity is *buithi*.

X. FURTHER READING

Now that you have finished this book (or are working hard on doing so), I hope you are hungry for more! Here are some useful books and articles that can help you get started. Once you have worked your way through these, start on the bibliographies you can find in the back of the books below. After you have finished those, get back to me…

Breatnach, Liam. 1977. 'The suffixed pronouns in early Irish'. In: *Celtica* 12: 75-105.

-----. 1980. 'Some remarks on the relative in Old Irish'. In: *Ériu* 31: 1-9.

Green, Antony. 1995. *Old Irish verbs and vocabulary*. Somerville.

McCone, Kim. 1996. *Towards a relative chronology of ancient and medieval Celtic sound change*. Maynooth Studies in Celtic Linguistics 1.   Maynooth.

-----. 1997. *The early Irish verb*. Maynooth Monographs 1. Second   edition. Maynooth.

-----. 2005. *A first Old Irish grammar and reader including an introduction to Middle Irish*. Maynooth Medieval Irish Texts III. Maynooth.

McCone, Kim et al.. 1994. *Stair na Gaeilge in ómós do Pádraig Ó Fiannachta*. Maynooth.

Pedersen, Holger, 1909-13. *Vergleichende Grammatik der keltischen Sprachen*, 2 vols. Göttingen.

Lewis, Henry and Holger Pedersen, 1937. *A concise comparative Celtic grammar*. Göttingen.

Quin, E.G. 1975. *Old-Irish Workbook*. Dublin: Royal Irish Academy.

Schrijver, Peter. 1997. *Studies in the history of Celtic pronouns and particles*. Maynooth Studies in Celtic Linguistics 2. Maynooth.

Stifter, David. 2006. *Sengoídelc. Old Irish for beginners.* Syracuse.

Strachan, John. 1904. 'The infixed pronoun in Middle Irish'. In: *Ériu* 1: 153-79.

-----. 1949. *Old-Irish paradigms and selections from the Old-Irish glosses.* Dublin: Royal Irish Academy.

Thurneysen, Rudolf. 1946. *A grammar of Old Irish. Revised and enlarged edition translated from the German by D.A. Binchy and Osborn Bergin. With supplement.* Dublin: Dublin Institute for Advanced Studies. If you can read German, I also recommend reading the original.

Tigges, Wim, in collaboration with Feargal Ó Béarra. 2006. *An Old Irish primer.* Nijmegen: Stichting Uitgeverij de Keltische Draak.

XI. INDEX

absolute (verb), 8, 69-70, 76-7, 91, 94-107, 109, 111-12, 115-19, 121-2, 124, 126, 128-30, 133, 136-7, 144, 148-9, 157-60, 163-5

accusative (case), 11, 13, 15-47, 50-1, 53, 57-8, 64, 71, 80-3, 87, 161

active voice (verb), 89-91, 93-4, 96, 98-102, 104-5, 110, 116-19, 121-2, 124, 126-8, 131, 144-6, 160, 165

adjective 7, 12, 47-58, 62-3, 82, 139-40, 150, 155, 157; irregular forms 57; adjective prefixed to nouns/verbs 49 *see also* attributive adjective, predicative adjective (under predicate)

adverb 12, 48, 58, 150, 152-3, 162; adverb formation 58; adverbs of place 58

anaphoric pronoun *s(u)ide* (pronoun) 66, 80

antecedent (relative clauses) 85, 87, 142-4, 147-51, 158

***ā*-preterite** (verb) 131

article 12, 14-21, 24, 48, 58, 60, 63, 81-2, 85-8; article + preposition, 19-21; double article rule 19

***ā*-stem** (noun) 28-31, 35, 49-51

***ā*-subjunctive** (verb) 90, 115-17, 119-21, 123-5

attributive adjective 48

augmented preterite (verb) 91, 129, 130, 131, 137, 165 *see also* perfect, preterite stem ac-tive, preterite stem passive, *ro*

augmenting particles, other than *ro* 139

***beirid*-group** (verb) *see* strong verbs
***benaid*-group** (verb) *see* strong verbs

cardinals (numerals) 59-61

case 11-46, 48, 50-8, 60-4 *see also* accusative, dative, genitive, nominative, vocative

cleft sentence 67, 147, 152-4

comparative (adjective) 54-7, 151 *see also* degrees of comparison

compensatory lengthening 41, 109, 131

compound verb 69, 77, 90-1, 106-9, 111, 113-14, 134, 136-8, 148-9

compound word with adjective 49; with numerals 62, 65

conditional (verb) 91, 122-5, 144, 160, 164

conjunct (verb) 90, 91, 95-100, 102, 104, 106-12, 115, 117-9, 121-31, 133-6, 138-9, 147-50, 156-65

conjunct particle 69-71, 83, 90-1, 95, 97, 107-8, 111, 131, 133-6, 138-9, 144, 147-8, 156-7, 161-4

conjunction 75, 114, 150

consonant 1-8, 15-17, 22-6, 28-35, 37-8, 40-7, 50-1, 68, 71, 73, 79-82, 93-4, 96-100, 102, 109, 111, 113, 115-18, 123-4, 126, 130-1, 136, 138-40, 165

consonant color/quality 3-5

consonantal stems (noun) 22, 37-47

copula (verb) 48, 53-4, 56, 66, 79-80, 149, 152-3, 155-9, 161

dative (case) 6, 11-13, 15-47, 50-2, 54-5, 57, 59-61, 63, 72, 77, 80, 81-2, 87, 141, 156; independent dative 12

degrees of comparison (adjective) 53-7 *see also* equative, comparative, superlative

deictic particle *í* 85-7

delenition 8, 15-7, 102-3, 119, 129

demonstrative 85, 87-8; used independently 88

dental stem (noun) 37, 40-1, 44-7, 61, 109, lenited 40-1, unlenited 41

dental stem (adjective) 49

dependent verbal form 68-9, 72, 90-1, 95, 101, 112, 132, *see also* conjunct, prototonic

deponent (verb), 89-90, 92, 96-8, 101, 109, 111, 118-19, 121, 127, 129, 131, 146

deuterotonic (verb) 69, 91, 94, 107-9, 112-13, 131-2, 137, 149 *see also* independent verbal form, absolute

devoicing 103, 109

diphthong 3, 22, 28-9, 53, 118, 131

direct object *see* object

double article rule *see* article

dual (number) 12, 16-18, 22-48, 55, 60, 89 *see also* number, plural, singular

ē-future (verb) 120, 123, 125

emphasizing pronoun 66-7, 78-9, 87

equative (adjective) 53-4, 56-7 *see also* degrees of comparison

feminine (gender) 9, 12, 17, 18 20-2, 28-45, 48, 50-2, 59-63, 71-3, 79, 82-6, 140 *see also* gender

f-future (verb) 90, 120-3

fractions (numerals) 63

future (verbal stem) 76, 90, 91, 110, 113-15, 120-8, 130, 132, 135, 144-6, 159, 164

gaibid-group (verb) *see* strong verb

gender 11-12, 14, 22, 48, 52, 67, 82-3, 140 *see also* feminine, masculine, neuter

genitive (case) 4, 7, 11, 14-20, 22-47, 51-2, 56-7, 60-1, 82-3, 141, 150, 153; objective genitive 141

gerundive, *see* verbal of necessity

glide vowel 5, 23, 33, 94, 118

guttural stem (noun), 37-40, lenited 39, unlenited 39-40

habitual present (substantive verb) 163

hiatus 3-4, 39, 57, 61, 63

hiatus verb 93, 104-6, 114, 120, 128, 161

h-mutation 4, 7, 9, 15-18, 20-1, 28-30, 32-8, 50, 73-5, 78

i, see deictic particle *i*

iā-stems (noun) 29-31, 49, 51

imperative (verb) 10, 75, 91, 111-14, 133, 159, 163-4

imperfect indicative (verb) 91, 110-11, 113, 116-17, 119, 122, 127, 135, 144, 158, 160, 163

independent dative *see* dative

independent pronoun 10, 66-8, 79, 152

independent verbal form 68-9, 90-1 112, 144, 160, 165 *see also* absolute, deuterotonic

indirect object *see* object

infixed pronoun 66, 68-79, 87, 95, 113, 134, 162 after *ná/nád* 75, 113; class A 68, 70-1, 73-5, 134, 162 ; class B 68, 73-5; class C 68, 74-5, 104, 134

interrogative particle 75, 90, 113, 134, 156

interrogative pronoun 66, 83-4

intransitive verb 96

io,iā-stem (adjective) 49, 51, 62, 65, 82, 139

io-stem (noun) 26-9

ī-preterite (verb) 131

ī-stem (noun) 31-2

i-stem (adjective) 49, 51-2

i-stem (noun) 32-35

leniting relative clause 147-8

lenition 2, 7-8, 14-17, 20-1, 23-47, 48, 50-2, 60, 70-1, 73, 78, 102-3, 119,

imperative, imperfect indicative, present indicative, strong verbs, weak verbs

preterite, 90-1, 110, 113, 115, 127-33, 135-9, 144-6, 158, 160, 165 *see also ā*-preterite, *i*-preterite, preterite stem active, preterite stem passive, reduplicated preterite, suffixless preterite, suppletive verbs, *t*-preterite; augmented preterite

preterite stem active (verb) 91, 110, 127-32, 144-6, 160

preterite stem passive (verb) 91, 110, 132-3, 139, 145

preverbal particle 136-9

pronouns, 10, 66-84, 150; *see also* anaphoric pronoun, emphasizing pronoun, independent pronoun, infixed pronoun, personal pronoun, possessive pronoun, suffixed pronoun

prototonic (verb) 69, 83, 91, 95 108-9, 112-3, 131-2, 134, 137-8, 149, 156 *see also* conjunct, dependent verbal forms

reduplicated future (verb) based on *ā*-subjunctive 123-5, *s*-future 126

reduplicated preterite (verb) 128, 130, 165

reduplication 123, 126, 128, 130-1, 165

relative particle *a* 75, 151

relative clause 68, 74-5, 83, 85, 113, 142-54, 158

ro (augmenting particle) 101, 129-31, 135-9, 160; fixed *ro* 139; meanings and usage of *ro* 135; movable *ro*, 138; position of *ro*, 136-9; preverbal *ro*, 138-9; pre-vocalic *ro* 138-9; *see also* augmented preterite, aug-menting particles other than *ro*, perfect

r-stem (noun) 37, 42-4, 65

secondary future *see* conditional

simple verb 69, 76-7, 90-1, 93-109, 111, 113, 134, 136, 144, 148-9

singular (number) 4, 7, 10, 12, 14-18, 20-47, 49-52, 54-5, 58-9, 61, 64, 66-7, 70-83, 85-6, 89, 94-106, 109-22, 124-6, 128-31, 133, 137-8, 141, 145-7, 149, 151, 156-65

s-**future** (verb) *see* reduplicated future

s-**preterite** (verb) 90, 128-30

s-**stem** (noun) 37, 43-7, masculine 44-5, neuter 46-7

s-**subjunctive** (verb) 114, 117-20, 126, 128, 145

stress 2-3, 6-7, 9, 41, 49, 59, 68-9, 107-9, 131, 136-9, 157

strong verb 90, 92, 98-101, 103-4, 107, 112, 114, 117, 120, 123, 125-6, 128-30, 133; *beirid*-group 91-2, 99-100, 106-7, 109, 111-13, 115-17, 129, 145; *benaid*-group 92, 101, 103-4, 112, 115, 120, 145; *gaibid*-group 92, 100-3, 112, 115

subject 10-11, 48, 67, 79-81, 83, 89-90, 94, 96, 140, 143, 151, 153-5, 157

subjunctive stem (verb) 10, 90-1, 110, 113-28, 135, 144-5, 159, 164 *see also ā*-subjunctive, *s*-subjunctive

substantive verb 155-6, 161-5

suffixed pronoun 66, 70, 76-8, 80

suffixless preterite (verb) 128, 130-1 *see also ā*-preterite, *i*-preterite, reduplicated preterite, suppletive verbs

superlative (adjective) 53, 56-7

suppletive verbs in future 120, 123, 127, in preterite 128, 132

syncope 5-6, 8, 31, 36, 38, 46, 56, 76-7, 108-9, 123-4, 126, 136-8

tense 10, 90-2, 96, 110, 113-15, 120, 127-8, 132-3, 135, 139, 144-5, 148, 161, 163

t-**preterite** 128-9, 132

transitive verb 96

u-**stem** (adjective) 49

u-**stem** (noun) 11, 35-7, 140

171

verb 3, 6, 8, 9-12, 29, 48-9, 54-5, 57, 66-77, 79-142, 144-65 *see also* copula, strong verbs, substantive verb, weak verbs

verbal adjective (past participle) 139-40

verbal noun (noun) 140-1, 150, 153, 156, 161, 165

verbal of necessity (also called gerundive; verb) 140, 165

vocalic stems (noun) 22-37

vocative (case) 11, 15, 22-48, 50-1, 89

voice, *see* active, deponent, passive

weak verbs 90, 92-8, 104, 107, 112, 114, 118, 120, 123, 128, 140

word order 11, 155

ABOUT THE AUTHOR

Ranke de Vries is a lecturer in Celtic Languages and Culture at Utrecht University. After obtaining her propedeutic diploma in Greek and Latin Languages and Culture from Radboud University Nijmegen, the Netherlands, she obtained M.A. degrees in Celtic Languages and Culture and Medieval Studies from Utrecht University, the Netherlands. She then completed her Ph.D. degree, an edition of two texts relating to the origin of Lough Neagh, at Trinity College Dublin under the supervision of Liam Breatnach and Damian McManus in 2007.

CPSIA information can be obtained at www.ICGtesting.com
Printed in the USA
LVOW13s0219170714

394635LV00030B/1322/P